FAITH THAT ENDURES

IN TIMES LIKE THESE

BIBLE STUDY GUIDE

From the Bible-teaching ministry of

Charles R. Swindoll

INSIGHT FOR LIVING

Charles R. Swindoll is a graduate of Dallas Theological Seminary and has served as senior pastor of the First Evangelical Free Church of Fullerton, California, since 1971. Chuck's radio program, "Insight for Living," began in 1979. In addition to his church and radio ministries, Chuck enjoys writing. He has authored numerous books and booklets on a variety of subjects.

Based on the outlines and transcripts of Chuck's sermons, the study guide text is co-authored by Lee Hough, a graduate of the University of Texas at Arlington and Dallas Theological Seminary. He also wrote the Living Insights sections.

Editor in Chief:
Cynthia Swindoll

Coauthor of Text:
Lee Hough

Assistant Editor:
Wendy Peterson

Copy Editors:
Deborah Gibbs
Cheryl Gilmore
Karene Wells

Designer:
Gary Lett

Publishing System Specialist:
Bob Haskins

Director, Communications Division:
Deedee Snyder

Manager, Creative Services:
Alene Cooper

Project Supervisor:
Susan Nelson

Print Production Manager:
John Norton

Printer:
Sinclair Printing Company

Unless otherwise identified, all Scripture references are from the New American Standard Bible, © The Lockman Foundation 1960, 1962, 1963, 1968, 1971, 1972, 1973, 1975, 1977. Used by permission. Other translations cited are the Amplified Bible [AMPLIFIED] and The Living Bible [LB].

An effort has been made to locate sources and obtain permission where necessary for the quotations used in this book. In the event of any unintentional omission, a modification will gladly be incorporated in future printings.

ISBN 0-8499-8441-6
Printed in the United States of America.

COVER DESIGN: Diana Vasquez
COVER PHOTOGRAPH: Tony Stone Worldwide

CONTENTS

INTRODUCTION

We are fast becoming a hang-loose, bail-out, run-away-from-it-all society. The old "tough it out" philosophy of the pioneer days is rarely found in our world of shallow roots and conditional commitments. Look around. Judge for yourself.

But God's people march to a different drummer—or, at least, we *should*. The underlying tone of Scripture is one of endurance, not escape . . . refusing to run, not looking for an easy way out. That's what this series is all about. It offers a muscular message that includes some sweat and tears. It does not promise a dreamy, fragrant rose garden but rather a strong exhortation to walk a consistent walk of discipline. Our faith needs fiber if we plan to do battle with age-old enemies like indifference and passivity. A stand must be taken if we hope to finish the course victoriously.

To borrow three questions from the eighteenth-century Isaac Watts, are you a soldier of the cross? A follower of the Lamb? Do you hope to be carried to the skies on flowery beds of ease? No! There are foes to face in this world that is no friend to grace. Hopefully each one of these chapters will encourage you to endure. Times like these demand such resolve.

Chuck Swindoll

Chuck Swindoll

PUTTING TRUTH
INTO ACTION

Knowledge apart from application falls short of God's desire for His children. He wants us to apply what we learn so that we will change and grow. This study guide was prepared with these goals in mind. As you go through the following pages, we hope your desire to discover biblical truth will grow as your understanding of God's Word increases, and that you will be encouraged to apply what you've learned.

To assist you in your study, we've included a section called *Living Insights* at the end of each lesson. These exercises will challenge you to study further and to think of specific ways to put your discoveries into action.

There are many ways to use this guide—in personal devotions, group studies, discussions with friends and family, and Sunday school classes. And, of course, it's an ideal study aid when you're listening to its corresponding "Insight for Living" radio series.

To benefit most from this study guide, we would encourage you to consider it a spiritual journal. That's why we've included space in the *Living Insights* for recording your thoughts and discoveries. We hope you'll return to those sections often for review and encouragement as you continue to grow in your walk with Christ.

Lee Hough
Coauthor of Text
Author of Living Insights

FAITH THAT ENDURES

IN TIMES LIKE THESE

Chapter 1

HOW TO STOP SHRINKING

Hebrews 10:32–39

Have you read the 'Faith Notices' in today's paper?"

"No, why?"

"Richard King—he's gone, quits, washed out."

"The evangelist Richard King? But he was just here; I heard him preach. He spoke as if he'd never been closer to the Lord. You're kidding."

"I wish I were. Here, read about it yourself."

FAITH NOTICES

BELLMAN, JANECE, 32, author of best-selling book *Discovering Christ's Joy* was arrested on July 9 for possession of cocaine. She was attending a Christian booksellers' convention where she was one of the keynote speakers. Cause of fall—stress.

LORAY, REV. JOHN, 53, was forced to resign his fourteen-year pastorate when it was discovered that he was addicted to pornography. Cause of fall—sexual immorality.

KING, RICHARD, 36, evangelist, admitted on June 15 to having an affair for the past three years with a member of his crusade staff. Richard King Ministries is also under indictment for tax fraud and misappropriation of funds. Cause of fall—immorality and greed.

WILER, MELISSA, 19, beloved daughter of Will and Susan Wiler, former active church member. Last

Tuesday denied having ever believed. Has left home and is currently living with her boyfriend. Cause of fall—drifted from the faith during first year of college.

———◆———

In reality, of course, there are no such things as "Faith Notices" for fallen believers. The names and circumstances listed are fictional. But, then, they're not really—not completely. Haven't we all heard of examples like these on the national news, local radio stations, in churches, or among friends? And not just once or twice, mind you, but again and again.

All around us, Christians of every age and occupation are dropping out of the race set before them as followers of Christ. Oftentimes, these are individuals who explode out of their conversions at full speed amidst cheers and adulation for their spiritual prowess. But soon their breathing becomes labored, and their faith begins to weaken. Bible study and prayer become a strain. They grow weary of life's relentless hurdles. Some stumble and fall, bringing others down with them; others simply slow to a walk and then drop out altogether, disgracing not only themselves but also the Savior they represent.

The apostle Paul once wrote,

> Do you not know that those who run in a race all run, but only one receives the prize? Run in such a way that you may win. (1 Cor. 9:24)

The key to winning the spiritual race Paul speaks of is not speed—it's endurance, obedience, staying faithful to the finish. That's winning. Is your faith strong enough to go the distance? Does it have the endurance to run the course of a lifetime?

Faith That Endures . . . in Times like These is a study designed to help train your faith to win. Whether you've just begun the race or are completing your twentieth year, here are eight chapters of biblical coaching and encouragement that will firm up your faith to press on—all the way to the finish line.

Three Categories of Faith

To begin, the first thing we need to firm up is our understanding of the word *faith*, which is mentioned more than two hundred times in the Scriptures. Broken down, the diverse biblical meanings of

2

this word can be divided into three basic categories.

Saving Faith

When the Philippian jailer asked Paul and Silas the straight-forward question, "Sirs, what must I do to be saved?" they replied, "Believe in the Lord Jesus, and you shall be saved" (Acts 16:30–31). That's saving faith, the kind Paul talks about in his letter to the Ephesians:

> For by grace you have been saved through faith; and that not of yourselves, it is the gift of God; not as a result of works, that no one should boast. (2:8–9; see also Rom. 5:1; Gal. 3:26)

Throughout Scripture, the clear, consistent message is that no one receives salvation except through faith in Jesus Christ alone (see also John 11:25–26; 14:6).

Doctrinal Faith

Faith is also used in Scripture to refer to the fundamental doctrinal truths and beliefs of Christianity. Jude, for example, gives the exhortation,

> Beloved, while I was making every effort to write you about our common salvation, I felt the necessity to write to you appealing that you contend earnestly for the faith which was once for all delivered to the saints. (v. 3; see also 1 Cor. 16:13; Col. 2:6–7)

Practical, Daily Faith

This category of faith has to do with relying on God, not self, in our everyday living. Paul succinctly expresses this type of practical faith in his second letter to the Corinthians, saying,

> For we walk by faith, not by sight. (5:7; see also Rom. 4:19–21)

In his letter to the Ephesians, the Apostle instructs us to battle spiritual forces of wickedness by putting on the armor of God, which includes

> taking up the shield of faith with which you will be able to extinguish all the flaming missiles of the evil one. (6:16b)

3

The only way to extinguish Satan's fiery arrows is with the shield of a daily, personal walk by faith. To find out more about how we can build up such an enduring, practical faith, let's turn to Hebrews 10, where the author explains how to keep from shrinking back in the midst of some very tough times.

Exhortation: Two Groups of Christians

To better understand the content of the letter to the Hebrews, let's examine the broader context of the day in which it was written.

According to scholars, Hebrews was written in A.D. 64, when the infamous Nero was emperor of Rome. On July 18 of that year, a fire raged through the imperial city, killing thousands. To remove suspicion from himself, Nero blamed the Christians and started a bloodthirsty campaign to purge them from his empire. John Fox, in his well-respected *Book of Martyrs*, writes:

> The barbarities exercised on the Christians were such as even excited the commiseration of the Romans themselves. Nero even refined upon cruelty, and contrived all manner of punishments for the Christians that the most infernal imagination could design. In particular, he had some sewed up in skins of wild beasts, and then worried by dogs until they expired; and others dressed in shirts made stiff with wax, fixed to axletrees, and set on fire in his gardens, in order to illuminate them. This persecution was general throughout the whole Roman Empire.[1]

The Christians who received the letter we're about to study obviously faced a depth of persecution and pain few of us will ever know. But we can know and enter into the advice offered by the author of Hebrews for strengthening our faith in tough times.

Those Who Stand

Beginning in verse 32, the writer gives three directives for standing firm. First, *remember previous victories.*

But remember the former days, when, after being

1. William Byron Forbush, ed., *Fox's Book of Martyrs* (Grand Rapids, Mich.: Zondervan Publishing House, 1967), p. 6.

4

enlightened, you endured a great conflict of sufferings.

When their spirits needed lifting, the Hebrews were to recall how God had enabled them to endure past times of hardship. Every act of God's goodness and grace—a need met, a specific victory, a time of comfort—was to be collected in a scrapbook of remembrances that would encourage the Hebrews in their present difficulties.

The author then reminds his readers of how they had suffered in the past, and why.

> Partly, by being made a public spectacle through reproaches and tribulations, and partly by becoming sharers with those who were so treated. For you showed sympathy to the prisoners, and accepted joyfully the seizure of your property, knowing that you have for yourselves a better possession and an abiding one. (vv. 33–34)

When they first became believers, these Jewish converts immediately experienced persecution by being ridiculed and tormented in public for their open and bold faith. They also endured other sufferings, including having their homes and belongings taken from them because they had cared for prisoners and others who were mistreated. But they accepted it joyfully. Why? Because they were walking by faith—a daily, practical, unquenchable belief that God had a better and lasting prize awaiting them. Their hopeful, trusting focus provided an anchor for their faith.

The second piece of advice is to *endure with boldness and confidence*.

> Therefore, do not throw away your confidence, which has a great reward. (v. 35)

The common temptation we all face in difficult times is to run away, to escape. But the writer exhorts us to do just the opposite. Instead of throwing away our confidence, we are to stay rooted and to endure. Such a response has a great reward, but, as we're reminded in verse 36, we must first have the faith to stand firm.

> For you have need of endurance, so that when you have done the will of God, you may receive what was promised.

The Greek term used here for *endurance* comes from two words:

5

hupo, meaning "under," and *menō*, "to abide." Combined, it conveys the idea of remaining patient, still, and confident in the Lord under the load of whatever burden He may want you to shoulder. The author knew his readers were going to need that kind of enduring faith, certainly to hold up under Nero's persecutions.

Quoting the Old Testament prophet Habakkuk, the writer's third instruction is to *exercise the faith within you.*

> For yet in a very little while,
> He who is coming will come, and will not delay.
> But My righteous one shall live by faith.
> (vv. 37–38a)

"My righteous one shall live by faith." As unusual as it may sound, those who suffer persecution don't need more faith nor even new faith to help them endure. Rather, they need to exercise the faith they already have. Marathon runners know that it's not more or new muscles they need, it's training the ones they already have that makes the difference. In the same way, only through stretching ourselves daily to trust in the Lord will we build up our spiritual strength and endurance.

Those Who Shrink

When every test arrives, we are faced with the decision to either stand or shrink. For those who seek to escape instead of endure, the author of Hebrews makes this sobering observation:

> And if he shrinks back, My soul has no plea-
> sure in him.
> But we are not of those who shrink back to destruc-
> tion, but of those who have faith to the preserving
> of the soul. (vv. 38b–39)

Two things are true of people who shrink back instead of standing firm. First, God takes no pleasure in them. And second, their lives become mired in misery. The most miserable Christians on earth are the ones who live by sight, who try to run the spiritual race set before them by trusting in their own flesh rather than in God.

Application

On the following page is a diagram to help you remember the truths highlighted in our study.

Beginning of Test	Period of Waiting	End of Test
Faith Challenged	Faith Strengthened	Faith Rewarded

At the beginning of every test, our faith is challenged. And at the end of each test, our faith is rewarded—God brings maturity, for example, or an answer is found, or peace is imparted. Before we receive that reward, however, we must first endure a period of waiting, where our faith is strengthened. It may last for a day, a month, or even years. The lesson to remember is this: Faith will never grow strong apart from endurance.

Living Insights

A young boy ran a race. Nothing unusual about that, boys and girls race all the time . . .

"On your mark."

. . . in backyards, across school yards, and around tracks.

"Get set."

What made this sprint special, one he would never forget, is that he finished.

"Go!"

Before the race ever began, he knew he couldn't win. But that's not what troubled him. It's where he would finish in the pack that mattered. After the first curve, he was running near the front. Down the straightaway, he settled into a respectable position in the middle. Around the second curve, he dropped a little farther back. By the end of the first lap—he was dead last.

Another lap to go and already a gap had opened between himself and the others charging ahead. With jagged, desperate breaths, he willed himself not to be left behind and humiliated, but his legs had nothing left to give. He could have faked a cramp and fallen down or suddenly "pulled a hamstring" and limped off the track; but he chose, instead, to stay in the race.

Out of the last curve and into the homestretch—no other runner in sight. They'd all finished. He could measure his own feelings of insignificance by the interminable time and yardage it took to run through that final gauntlet of jeers to the finish line.

"Hurry up, Flash!"

"Get off the track, ya slug!"

Laughter.

Five more yards.

More taunting.

Finish line.

The young boy didn't know it then, but years later, looking back as a man, he realized that had been one of the best races he ever ran. It was more than a simple test of speed. He had competed against the deeper, more difficult opponents of humiliation, pain, and the temptation to quit. And he won. He endured to overcome them all and cross the finish line.

Are you running against those same competitors in your race to remain faithful to Christ? We all do, and they have caused many to stumble and fall. Even now they may be slowing you down, tempting you to quit. But remember the young boy. Remember that winning isn't about speed, it's about enduring—staying faithful around the curves, down the straightaways, when you're running all alone or in a pack, when people jeer you or cheer you. It's about keeping your focus on Christ all the way to the finish line.

Remember, too, that you're not alone. Jesus is there to strengthen and encourage you, all of heaven is rooting for you, and, though you may not see him, there's a young boy in the stands who's cheering madly for you too.

Living Insights

As a way of warming up for the studies ahead, set aside some time to examine your own spiritual track record. Have there been times when your faith was seriously injured and you thought about dropping out? What about times when your faith felt strong? Using the space provided, write out a general description of the straightaways and curves your faith has endured since you first became a Christian.

My Race of Faith

Straightaways _____

_____

_____

Curves

9

Chapter 2

PROFILE OF A FAITH THAT ENDURES

Hebrews 11:1–6

To enjoy the water-lilied canvases of Claude Monet, you must visit the Musée de l'Orangerie in Paris. If you want to gaze at Michelangelo's *The Creation of Adam*, you must travel to the Vatican's Sistine Chapel in Rome. Or if you are interested in viewing William Holman Hunt's compelling *The Light of the World*, you would need to go to Keble College in Oxford.

If, however, you want to see a classic portrait of enduring faith inspired by the Master Himself, you must turn to the Hall of Faith in Hebrews 11. There, hanging in the entryway, you'll find these immortal words:

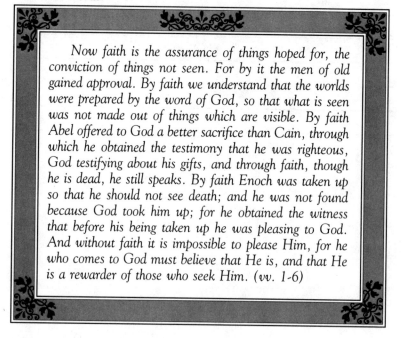

> *Now faith is the assurance of things hoped for, the conviction of things not seen. For by it the men of old gained approval. By faith we understand that the worlds were prepared by the word of God, so that what is seen was not made out of things which are visible. By faith Abel offered to God a better sacrifice than Cain, through which he obtained the testimony that he was righteous, God testifying about his gifts, and through faith, though he is dead, he still speaks. By faith Enoch was taken up so that he should not see death; and he was not found because God took him up; for he obtained the witness that before his being taken up he was pleasing to God. And without faith it is impossible to please Him, for he who comes to God must believe that He is, and that He is a rewarder of those who seek Him. (vv. 1-6)*

A Detailed Description

To increase our appreciation of this profile of faith, let's step closer and look more fully at the depth and meaning portrayed in these six verses.

Five Observations

As we examine each bold stroke and delicate shading, we can make five important observations.

First: *Faith involves assurance and conviction* (v. 1). The word *assurance* in verse 1 comes from the term meaning "to stand under." According to commentator Leon Morris,

> it is used of that which underlies the surface appearance, that which makes a thing what it is. Faith is that which "stands under" our hopes. What we hope for is not present with us now, but that does not mean that we may not be certain about it. Christians are certain, for example, of their eternal salvation, though they do not yet see it in all its fullness. What gives certainty is faith. It is all we have at present and it is all we need. It undergirds the Christian life.[1]

Faith is also characterized by conviction, which means certainty. "To the writer to the Hebrews," notes commentator William Barclay,

> faith is absolutely certain that what it believes is true and that what it expects will come. It is not the hope which looks forward with wistful longing; it is the hope which looks forward with utter conviction. In the early days of persecution they brought a humble Christian before the judges. He told them that nothing they could do could shake him because he believed that, if he was true to God, God would be true to him. "Do you really think," asked the judge, "that the like of you will go to God and his glory?" "I do not think," said the man, "I know."[2]

1. Leon Morris, *Hebrews*, Bible Study Commentary Series (Grand Rapids, Mich.: Zondervan Publishing House, 1983), p. 104. In extrabiblical writings, *assurance* was also used to refer to a title that documents ownership of property, which is why some have translated this verse, "Faith is the *title-deed* of things hoped for." See F. F. Bruce, *The Epistle to the Hebrews* (1964; reprint, Grand Rapids, Mich.: William B. Eerdmans Publishing Co., 1988), p. 278.

2. William Barclay, *The Letter to the Hebrews*, rev. ed., The Daily Study Bible Series (Philadelphia, Pa.: Westminster Press, 1976), p. 128. The faith Moses exercised is an outstanding example of assurance and conviction (see Heb. 11:24–29).

Second: *Faith always relates to things yet future* (v. 1). "Faith is the assurance of things *hoped for*" (emphasis added). The word *hope* always points to the future. Faith is the cement we mix into hope to harden it into assurance and conviction. Without it, our hope is little more than a slush of wishful thinking.

Third: *Faith has as its object "things not seen"* (vv. 1b, 3). Heaven, the resurrection of loved ones, a new life in Christ, even Jesus Himself—all these are out of the range of our physical vision. But when we focus the eyes of our heart on these unseen things, we develop an incredible ability to see not only what God has done and is doing in our lives, but also those things He will one day make visible in eternity.

Fourth: *Faith is basic to pleasing God* (vv. 2, 6a). By faith we gain the approval of God, as Enoch did (v. 5). Nothing substitutes for faith when it comes to pleasing Him. No amount of good works, of sacrifice, of religious activity can make up for what is lacking in our faith.

Fifth: *Faith means focusing fully on God* (v. 6b). It is so easy to let our faith slip away as we let God slip from our view. To fight against this, ask yourself, Could someone conclude that God exists by watching my life? Do my actions reveal that Jesus is alive and available for strength, wisdom, and encouragement? Another way of considering this same issue is to ask yourself, If God suddenly stopped existing, what difference would it make in my job? my home? my attitude?

Besides trusting in God's existence, true faith also affirms that He rewards those who seek Him (v. 6b). The Greek term used here for *seek* means "to search diligently, demand." There's an intensity in this word much like what you find in the way Jacob sought a blessing from his heavenly opponent in Genesis 32. In his meditation titled *The Magnificent Defeat*, Frederick Buechner paints a vivid picture of that encounter.

> Out of the deep of the night a stranger leaps. He hurls himself at Jacob, and they fall to the ground, their bodies lashing through the darkness. It is terrible enough not to see the attacker's face, and his strength is more terrible still, the strength of more than a man. All the night through they struggle in silence until just before morning when it looks as though a miracle might happen. Jacob is winning.

The stranger cries out to be set free before the sun rises. Then, suddenly, all is reversed.

He merely touches the hollow of Jacob's thigh, and in a moment Jacob is lying there crippled and helpless. The sense we have, which Jacob must have had, that the whole battle was from the beginning fated to end this way, that the stranger had simply held back until now, letting Jacob exert all his strength and almost win so that when he was defeated, he would know that he was truly defeated; so that he would know that not all the shrewdness, will, brute force that he could muster were enough to get this. Jacob will not release his grip, only now it is a grip not of violence but of need, like the grip of a drowning man.

The darkness has faded just enough so that for the first time he can dimly see his opponent's face. And what he sees is something more terrible than the face of death—the face of love. It is vast and strong, half ruined with suffering and fierce with joy, the face a man flees down all the darkness of his days until at last he cries out, "I will not let you go, unless you bless me!" Not a blessing that he can have now by the strength of his cunning or the force of his will, but a blessing that he can have only as a gift.[3]

The author of Hebrews calls this gift a reward. It is the sweet prize reserved only for those who diligently hold on to the Lord with all their attention and affection. When we focus fully on Him, we gain a greater glimpse of His power and presence. And our faith grows in proportion to the greatness of that glimpse.

Two Suggestions

Like all great works of art, God's timeless profile of faith evokes a response from its admirers. We may praise it, applaud it, recommend it to others; but to truly come to grips with its personal implications for our own lives, we need to follow two suggestions.

3. Frederick Buechner, *The Magnificent Defeat* (San Francisco, Calif.: HarperCollins Publishers, HarperSanFrancisco, 1966), pp. 17–18.

First: Ask yourself, *Why is faith such a struggle for me?* Is it because you fear that God won't come through? Or are you so filled with bitterness that there's no room for faith? Could it be that you are too proud to feel a need for God? Maybe it's insecurity—you feel that God doesn't really care, that He couldn't possibly be interested in somebody like you.

Why is faith such a struggle? Answer that question and you will have taken an important step toward removing a significant barrier to exhibiting the same kind of faith profiled in Hebrews 11.

And second: Do yourself a favor—*live one day at a time.* Why do so many of us live life like Montaigne, the Frenchman who said,

> My life has been full of terrible misfortunes, most of which never happened.[4]

John Haggai offers this plausible explanation in his book *How to Win Over Worry:*

> The trouble with many people is that instead of "looking to Jesus" they are looking to tomorrow.
> Yesterday is a cashed check and cannot be negotiated. Tomorrow is a promissory note and cannot be utilized today. Today is cash in hand. Spend it wisely. . . .
> Seize today. Live for today. Wring it dry of every opportunity.[5]

Learn to bite off life in daily chunks. Focus on today and don't be anxious about tomorrow, for as the Lord said: "Tomorrow will care for itself" (Matt. 6:34).

A Practical Summary

In our first lesson, we learned that faith is like a muscle and must be exercised, or it will atrophy. From this lesson, we can see that faith is like a sunrise, fresh every morning. Tomorrow's sun brings new opportunities for each of us to imitate that picture of enduring faith hanging in Hebrews 11. And as we apply the five observations from our study, a new profile will emerge in our spiritual lives, one that resembles the masterpiece—and the Master.

4. Michel Eyquemde de Montaigne, as quoted by John Edmund Haggai in *How to Win Over Worry* (Grand Rapids, Mich.: Zondervan Publishing House, 1959), p. 85.

5. Haggai, *How to Win Over Worry*, pp. 83, 87.

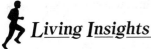

Living Insights

In his book *The Problem of Pain*, C. S. Lewis writes:

> We are, not metaphorically but in very truth, a Divine work of art, something that God is making, and therefore something with which He will not be satisfied until it has a certain character. Here again we come up against what I have called the "intolerable compliment." Over a sketch made idly to amuse a child, an artist may not take much trouble: he may be content to let it go even though it is not exactly as he meant it to be. But over the great picture of his life—the work which he loves, though in a different fashion, as intensely as a man loves a woman or a mother a child—he will take endless trouble—and would, doubtless, thereby *give* endless trouble to the picture if it were sentient. One can imagine a sentient picture, after being rubbed and scraped and re-commenced for the tenth time, wishing that it were only a thumb-nail sketch whose making was over in a minute. In the same way, it is natural for us to wish that God had designed for us a less glorious and less arduous destiny; but then we are wishing not for more love but for less.[6]

In the rubbing, scraping, and recommencing of your faith, are you wishing for less love instead of more? Are you leaning toward a lackluster, thumbnail sketch of faith instead of a gloriously enduring one?

Of the five observations drawn from the faith portrait in Hebrews 11:1–6, which one or two do you struggle with most? How?

_____

_____

_____

_____

6. C. S. Lewis, *The Problem of Pain* (New York, N.Y.: Macmillan Publishing Co., 1962), pp. 42–43.

This week, in what specific situations and ways can you exercise faith in these areas?

_____

_____

_____

_____

_____

🏃 Living Insights   STUDY TWO

In his insightful book *Principles of Spiritual Growth*, Miles J. Stanford states:

> True faith must be based solely on scriptural *facts*, for "faith cometh by hearing, and hearing by the word of God" (Rom. 10:17). Unless our faith is established on facts, it is no more than conjecture, superstition, speculation or presumption.
>
> . . . Faith standing on the facts of the Word of God substantiates and gives evidence of things not seen. And everyone knows that evidence must be founded on facts. . . .
>
> Since true faith is anchored on scriptural facts, we are certainly not to be influenced by *impressions*. George Mueller said, "Impressions have neither one thing nor the other to do with faith. Faith has to do with the Word of God. It is not impressions, strong or weak, which will make the difference. We have to do with the Written Word and not ourselves or our impressions."
>
> Then, too, *probabilities* are the big temptation when it comes to exercising faith. Too often the attitude is: "It doesn't seem probable that he will ever be saved." "The way things are going, I wonder if the Lord really loves me." But Mueller wrote: "Many people are willing to believe regarding those things that seem probable to them. Faith has nothing to do with probabilities. The province of faith

16

begins where probabilities cease and sight and sense fail. Appearances are not to be taken into account. The question is—whether God has spoken it in His Word."

Alexander R. Hay adds . . . "faith is not . . . a striving to believe that something shall be, thinking that if we believe hard enough it will come to pass." That may be positive thinking but certainly not biblical faith.[7]

Is there a situation in your life right now where, instead of exercising true faith, you're trusting in impressions, probabilities, or positive thinking? How would approaching this situation with true faith founded on the Word of God be different?

_____

_____

_____

_____

_____

What must you do to make this change?

_____

_____

_____

_____

_____

7. Miles J. Stanford, *Principles of Spiritual Growth* (Lincoln, Nebr.: Back to the Bible, 1977 ed.), pp. 7–8.

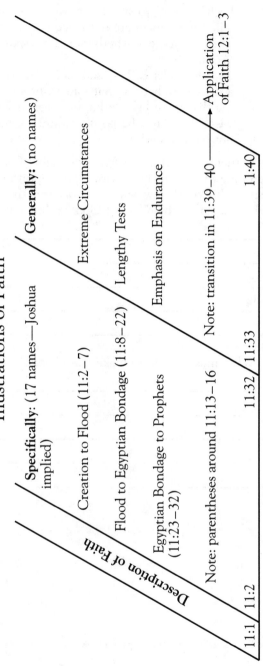

CHART OF HEBREWS 11

Key Verse: Hebrews 11:6

And without faith it is impossible to please Him, for he who comes to God must believe that He is, and that He is a rewarder of those who seek Him.

Illustrations of Faith

Specifically: (17 names—Joshua implied)

Generally: (no names)

Creation to Flood (11:2–7)

Flood to Egyptian Bondage (11:8–22)

Egyptian Bondage to Prophets (11:23–32)

Extreme Circumstances

Lengthy Tests

Emphasis on Endurance

Note: parentheses around 11:13–16

Note: transition in 11:39–40 ——▶ Application of Faith 12:1–3

Description of Faith

11:1 | 11:2   11:32 | 11:33   11:40

Chapter 3

LOOKING BACK: THEY PLEASED GOD

Hebrews 11:6–40

In Cologne, Germany, on the wall of a cellar where Jews hid from the Nazis, an inscription reads:

> I believe in the sun even when it is not shining.
> I believe in love even when feeling it not.
> I believe in God even when He is silent.[1]

A poignant reminder of enduring faith. Not some superficial optimism that loves to sing "My Faith Looks Up to Thee" only if a test doesn't last too long or cause too much inconvenience. No, this was real, lasting faith . . . something that seems so rare these days, so precious.

Is it because enduring faith is reserved only for monks and mystics who hear the audible voice of God? Or is it available to the ordinary citizens of heaven whose daily lives are taken up less with hearing God's voice than with hearing the cries of babies, the hum of computers, and the roar of crowded freeways?

The answer is found in Hebrews 11—and it may surprise you. More than that, it will encourage you.

Things Worth Noticing

Before we set foot in Hebrews 11, it will help if we first acquaint ourselves with the chapter's overall context, theme, and structure. The context was established back in chapter 10, where the author exhorted his readers to recall and be encouraged by how God enabled them to endure past sufferings (vv. 32–36). This would help them continue living by faith in the midst of their present difficulties, which, in a nutshell, was God's will for them: "But My righteous one shall live by faith" (v. 38a).

So the stage is now set for Hebrews 11, where the author offers

1. Nahum N. Glatzer, ed., *The Passover Haggadah* (New York, N.Y.: Schocken Books, 1989), p. xxvi.

more encouragement by bringing to mind numerous examples of Old Testament men and women who lived by faith.

The theme of chapter 11, which also originates in chapter 10, is the importance of enduring faith (vv. 36, 38). God takes pleasure in seeing His children endure rather than shrink back during difficult times.

As illustrated by the chart preceding this chapter, Hebrews 11 can be divided structurally into two sections. On the left side, verses 2–32 showcase seventeen men and women of faith whose lives extend chronologically from the time of Creation to the days of the prophets.[2] On the right side, beginning with verse 33 and continuing to the end of the chapter, a general description is given of great feats accomplished by faith and great suffering endured by faith.

Topics Worth Considering

With that background information behind us, we're ready to consider four important topics from Hebrews 11 that will answer the question posed at the beginning: Is it possible for all believers to cultivate an enduring faith, or is it just for specially gifted spiritual giants? Let's find out.

Faith . . . as It Relates to People

Doubtless, some of you who have read Hebrews 11 before may be thinking, "It's wonderful that all those people had the faith to do what they did; but me, well, I'm just not the faith type. I'm a career-oriented person. I make my living based on facts, not faith. God hasn't 'called' me to shut the mouths of any lions or perform great acts of righteousness, and He probably never will. I'm just not the minister type."

Sound familiar? If it does, here's an important principle for you to remember: No specific type qualifies. If you think a person has to be a certain type to live by faith, you've missed something crucial about the people mentioned in Hebrews 11. Take Abel, for example. He was just an ordinary herdsman, a "keeper of flocks" (Gen. 4:2). He never went to seminary, never was ordained, never preached in a pulpit. Noah was a farmer who took up shipbuilding for about 120 years of his life. Abraham was a businessman, and the list goes on:

2. Only sixteen names are specifically mentioned. However, Joshua is clearly implied in verse 30, making the total seventeen.

Sarah—homemaker
Joseph—slave, prisoner, prime minister
Moses—shepherd
Joshua—soldier
Gideon, Barak, and Samson—judges
David—shepherd, songwriter, outlaw, and king

These people had mostly common, ordinary, even undesirable backgrounds, and yet they all learned to live by faith. Occupation, sex, heredity, environment, color, economic status, age—none of these have anything to do with whether a person can qualify to live by faith.

Still, some of you may be thinking, "But you don't know my background. If you only knew the mistakes I've made, the sins I've committed, you'd know that I've got the wrong kind of track record for anybody to consider me as a man or woman of faith."

Oh, really? Don't count yourself out yet. Another important principle to remember is this: *No special record is necessary.* Look back over the names from Hebrews 11. Remember Noah? Yes, he built the ark and made it through the Flood. But what many people don't know is that he planted a vineyard shortly thereafter and got drunk. Abraham habitually lied about his wife, putting her in great jeopardy. And Sarah? She laughed when God told her she was going to have a baby. Not exactly a model response of faith. Then there's Jacob, the world-class chiseler, Moses the murderer, Rahab the harlot, and the sexually promiscuous Samson.

The point is, everyone's track record has blemishes, but that doesn't disqualify us from ever pleasing God. In each of the unique situations listed in this chapter, these people exercised the kind of faith described in verse 6, and it pleased God. Regardless of our shortcomings, we can still qualify as men and women of faith if we will exercise that same kind of faith in the unique circumstances of our own lives.

Faith . . . as It Relates to Circumstances

Already it should be clear that ordinary people can live extraordinary lives of faith. It wasn't Moses' background, Noah's skill, Sarah's age, or Rahab's reputation that entered each of them in the Hebrews 11 Hall of Faith; it was their enduring faith . . . a faith that illustrates for us the overwhelming odds against trusting in the Lord.

Once again, consider Noah's situation (11:7). Never before in history, short as it was to that time, had there ever been rain, much less a flood. Yet Noah continued day after day, month after month, year after year, measuring, sawing, dovetailing together a colossal contraption in his backyard, which had the whole countryside in stitches. Why did he persist? Because by faith in the Lord he could see "things not yet seen" (v. 7).

The odds weren't in Abraham's favor either when he uprooted his family to go to a land given to him by God, a land whose location was completely unknown to him (v. 8). Nor did anyone need to explain to Sarah the odds of having a baby at ninety years of age (v. 11). And what about the odds of parting a sea (v. 29), or of shouting down the fortified walls of a city (v. 30), or of any of the miraculous events recorded in verses 33–35a?

> Who by faith conquered kingdoms, performed acts of righteousness, obtained promises, shut the mouths of lions, quenched the power of fire, escaped the edge of the sword, from weakness were made strong, became mighty in war, put foreign armies to flight. Women received back their dead by resurrection.

Besides learning of the odds against our living by faith, we also learn from further examples given in Hebrews 11 that *the final outcome is not always pleasant.*

> Others were tortured, not accepting their release, in order that they might obtain a better resurrection; and others experienced mockings and scourgings, yes, also chains and imprisonment. They were stoned, they were sawn in two, they were tempted, they were put to death with the sword; they went about in sheepskins, in goatskins, being destitute, afflicted, ill-treated (men of whom the world was not worthy), wandering in deserts and mountains and caves and holes in the ground. (vv. 35b–38; see also vv. 13–14)

Now some might read this and think these people must not have been men and women of faith. But remember, verse 38 compliments them as being individuals "of whom the world was not worthy." Their faith was just as real and pleasing to God as Enoch's or David's. And their dire stories bring a balance to this chapter and to our understanding of what it means to live by faith: Faith doesn't necessarily change circumstances; it changes *us* so we can handle them. Faith may not keep a woman's husband from running away, for example, but it can give her the endurance she'll need to get through that difficult circumstance.

Faith . . . as It Relates to God

In addition to telling us how faith relates to people and circumstances, Hebrews 11 also reveals how God responds to our faith. For instance, *faith brings God pleasure.*

> Without faith it is impossible to please Him, for he who comes to God must believe that He is, and that He is a rewarder of those who seek Him. (v. 6)

When the Lord witnesses our willingness to trust Him, to wait on Him, to lean on Him as no other, it pleases Him. He's attracted to the kind of person depicted in 2 Chronicles 16:9a, which says,

> "For the eyes of the Lord move to and fro throughout the earth that He may strongly support those whose heart is completely His."

Not only does our faith please God, Hebrews 11:16 tells us *it also gives Him honor.*

> But as it is, they desire a better country, that is a heavenly one. Therefore God is not ashamed to be called their God.

Faith that endures brings honor to God. When the Lord says He is "the God of Abraham, Isaac, and Jacob," it shows that He is comfortable having His name associated with people who believe that He exists and that He will reward those who seek Him.

Faith . . . as It Relates to You

One final lesson we can draw from the heroes in Hebrews 11 is that God will use our faith as a testimony to Himself just as He did theirs. In His own time, He will place us on display and receive glory from us as He did with Abel (v. 4), Enoch (v. 5), and Noah (v. 7).

Truths Worth Remembering

Hebrews 11—what an encouraging chapter. We come away

with the assurance that, yes, it is possible for ordinary people like ourselves to live extraordinary lives of faith. We learn, too, some important insights about that faith as it relates to circumstances, God, and ourselves.

As we prepare to go and exercise that same faith exhibited by Noah, Sarah, and the rest, we need to remember two truths: First, *faith is not a substitute for wisdom and common sense.* Abraham left his country without knowing where he was headed because God called him to do so in a clear, audible voice (Gen. 12:1–3). That was faith. It's not faith, however, to pack the moving van with all your belongings and take off trusting that God will show you your next inheritance. That's presumption—presuming God will do something He never promised you in the first place.

Second, *the proper use of faith will turn your life right side up.* This means that you are living upside down if yours is not a life of faith. Using *faith* as an acrostic, here's a helpful reminder of some of the areas where we need to properly exercise our faith.

Finances
Attitudes
Ideas
Troubles
Home

Are you handling His money as a wise steward? Is your attitude based on sight or faith? Have you asked Him for some faith-filled ideas lately? Are troubles in your life producing enduring faith? Does your home life reflect the grace, truth, and love of the object of your faith—Jesus Christ?

Living Insights

From the time we were babies, most of us have been suckled on the idea of happy endings. "Happily ever after" was spoon-fed to us in bedtime stories and served up in the movies we watched. And if that weren't enough, plenty of preachers promise happy endings to our adult troubles if we will but have faith and be good little boys and girls.

The older we get, however, the more life has a tendency of knocking that nonsense right out of us. Difficult circumstances hit that no amount of faith can fend off. Think about those Christians mentioned in Hebrews 11 who were sawn in two, tortured, stoned, and forced to live like animals in caves. Men and women "of whom the world was not worthy" (v. 38). They had faith. And no doubt they prayed for deliverance and protection. But there was no happy-ever-after awaiting them. Only more mockings, pain, and finally death.

What do you do when the final outcome is not always pleasant? When, after earnest prayer, your spouse still walks away, your child dies, or your money doesn't come in? "Pain and suffering have happened—*now* what will you do?" writes Philip Yancey in his book *Where Is God When It Hurts?*

> Most of us expend our energy trying to figure out the cause of our pain before we'll decide how to respond. Joni Eareckson . . . consumed two years exploring possible causes of her accident. But, as Joni found, to the extent that we concentrate on cause, we may well end up embittered against God.
>
> . . . The real issue before Christians is not "Is God responsible?" but "How should I react now that this terrible thing has happened?"[3]

Is your faith being tested right now by circumstances that are anything but pleasant? What will you do? Focus on the cause, or on your response? What do you think would constitute a response of faith in your situation?

_____

_____

_____

_____

To strengthen your response of faith, on what aspect of God's character could you meditate? His sovereignty, perhaps? Or His compassion? In the following space, identify the character trait you wish to focus on; then look it up in a concordance or topical Bible, and write down the verses that encourage you. Finally, select one

3. Philip Yancey, *Where Is God When It Hurts?* (Grand Rapids, Mich.: Zondervan Publishing House, 1977), p. 85.

verse to memorize, and commit yourself to meditating on it for the rest of the day.

Character trait:_____

_____

_____

_____

Memory verse:_____

_____

_____

_____

🏃 *Living Insights* STUDY TWO

It's very odd. Exercising faith in tough times is crucial for developing an enduring faith—the Scriptures even say so (James 1:2–4). Yet many today are saying it's unspiritual not to live victoriously, free from all sickness and hardship. Philip Yancey comments:

> We seem to reserve our shiniest merit badges for those who have been healed, featuring them in magazine articles and TV specials, with the frequent side-effect of causing unhealed ones to feel as though God has passed them by. We make faith not an attitude of trust in something unseen but a route to get something *seen*—something magical and stupendous, like a miracle or supernatural gift. Faith includes the supernatural, but it also includes daily, dependent trust in spite of results. True faith implies a belief without solid proof—the evidence of things not seen, the substance of things hoped for. God is not mere magic.[4]

_____

4. Yancey, *Where Is God When It Hurts?*, p. 73.

A healed leg certainly glorifies God, but so does the unbroken faith of the individual whose leg is still crooked. Is that you? Are you exercising daily, dependent trust in spite of the results right now? Have all signs of the Savior's care and concern been removed from your world, and yet you're still believing? Far from being unspiritual, my friend, you're demonstrating a deep, genuine faith. One that pleases God and brings honor to His name. You are one of this world's true heroes, a man or a woman of whom the world is not worthy.

God bless you. . . .

Chapter 4
LIVING TODAY:
YOU CAN TOO!
Hebrews 12:1–3

Many of the world's greatest runners never won a gold medal, never set any records, never competed on a track, never donned a track shoe. But, oh, did they run. Think about a champion named Paul, who said,

> I have finished the course, I have kept the faith; in the future there is laid up for me the crown of righteousness, which the Lord, the righteous Judge, will award to me on that day; and not only to me, but also to all who have loved His appearing.
> (2 Tim. 4:7b–8)

Think about Amy Carmichael, whose great strides brought the love of Christ to India's outcasts.

> Love through me, Love of God . . .
> O Love that faileth not, break forth,
> And flood this world of Thine. . . .
>
> Pour through me now: I yield myself to Thee,
> Love, blessed Love, do as Thou wilt with me.[1]

Think about William Wilberforce's grueling parliamentary marathon to abolish England's slave trade.

> Never, never will we desist till we have wiped away this scandal from the Christian name, released ourselves from the load of guilt under which we at present labour, and extinguish every trace of this bloody traffic, of which our posterity, looking back

---

Certain sections of this chapter have been adapted from "Arena Lifestyle," in the study guide *The Practical Life of Faith*, coauthored by Ken Gire, from the Bible-teaching ministry of Charles R. Swindoll (Fullerton, Calif.: Insight for Living, 1989).

1. Amy Carmichael, *Toward Jerusalem*, pp. 11, 69, as quoted by Elisabeth Elliot in *Meet the Men and Women We Call Heroes*, ed. Ann Spangler and Charles Turner (Ann Arbor, Mich.: Servant Publications, Vine Books, 1983, 1985), p. 28.

to the history of these enlightened times, will scarce believe that it has been suffered to exist so long a disgrace and dishonour to this country.[2]

These were truly champions, gold medalists of faith who ran with endurance against formidable competition and cleared all the hurdles in their paths. Don't you wish you could run like that? Would you like to learn? It's not too late. What you need is some expert coaching and encouragement, and that's exactly what you'll receive in the training camp for long-distance runners that opens in Hebrews 12. Amy Carmichael trained there and so did William Wilberforce. How about you?

Witnesses of the Race

> Therefore, since we have so great a cloud of witnesses surrounding us . . . (12:1a)[3]

Camp officially opens with those spiritual athletes paraded in the previous chapter being ushered off the track and into the grandstands. All the saints who have finished the course, from Abel on, "are now waiting for the last runner to finish the race, and then the prizes will be given."[4] Now it is our turn to take hold of the baton of faith that has been handed off from generation to generation and "run with endurance the race that is set before us" (v. 1b).

The word translated "race" is from the Greek term *agōn*, from which we get the word *agony*. By choosing this word, the writer is picturing athletes in an agonizing footrace running for the finish line, all the while surrounded by the enduring examples of faith's heroes from past generations.

Do such all-stars as Enoch, Noah, Moses, and Sarah literally watch us run? Some commentators believe they do. However, the Greek term translated here as "witnesses" is the word for *testimony*. Rather than being surrounded by a great crowd of onlookers, the text suggests that we're surrounded by a great cloud of encouraging testimonies, which urge us to complete our leg of the race.

---

2. William Wilberforce, as quoted by Charles Colson in *Heroes*, ed. Spangler and Turner, p. 234.

3. The *therefore* of Hebrews 12:1 ties chapter 12 to chapter 11 in a cause-and-effect relationship. Consequently, the "cloud of witnesses surrounding us" refers to those in chapter 11, whose lives were such an eloquent testimony of faith.

4. M. R. De Haan, *Hebrews* (Grand Rapids, Mich.: Zondervan Publishing House, 1959), p. 164.

Preparing for the Race

Next, in verses 1b–3, the writer coaches us on how to get ready for the race and how to stay on track.

Things to Lay Aside

Before taking our places at the starting blocks, we're instructed to limber up by:

> lay[ing] aside every encumbrance, and the sin which
> so easily entangles us, and let us run with endurance
> the race that is set before us. (v. 1b)

The first tip we receive is to put aside anything and everything that might weigh us down and keep us from running well. An "encumbrance" is any excess weight. The Greek term from which we get this word literally means "mass" or "bulk." For a runner, this might be a set of heavy running weights or a pair of bulky sweatpants. For a Christian, it's anything that slows the pace in the progress of our faith: an indifferent attitude, a lack of mental discipline, procrastination, impatience, or a motley wardrobe of other things that should be boxed up and thrown away.

The second tip is to shed the "sin which so easily entangles us." What is this sin? The context of Hebrews 10–12 suggests it is the sin of unbelief, which affects us like a cramp in the leg, causing us to break our stride or hobble off the track altogether.

Instructions to Runners

The writer then goes on to tell us to "run with endurance the race that is set before us." The emphasis here is on endurance, the kind our coaching assistant William Barclay says

> does not mean the patience which sits down and
> accepts things but the patience which masters them.
> It is not some romantic thing which lends us wings
> to fly over the difficulties and the hard places. It is
> a determination, unhurrying and yet undelaying,
> which goes steadily on and refuses to be deflected.
> Obstacles do not daunt it and discouragements do
> not take its hope away. It is the steadfast endurance
> which carries on until in the end it gets there.[5]

5. William Barclay, *The Letter to the Hebrews*, rev. ed., The Daily Study Bible Series (Philadelphia, Pa.: Westminster Press, 1976), p. 173.

Focus While Running

In chapter 12, verse 2, the writer examines our stride and coaches us to keep our head up,

> *fixing* our eyes on Jesus, the author and perfecter of faith, who for the joy set before Him endured the cross, despising the shame, and has sat down at the right hand of the throne of God. (emphasis added)

Our Eyes

The first word in this verse is from the verb *aphoraō*. It means "to look away from all else and fix one's gaze upon." Greek scholar Brooke Foss Westcott comments on this present participle, suggesting that it means attention focused "not only at the first moment, but constantly during the whole struggle."[6]

And who is the one upon whom we are to have this intense, continual focus? Jesus, the author and perfecter of faith, the one who both started and finished the race.

Our Example

As runners, we must train our eyes on Christ. We shouldn't turn our heads to see where the other runners are, and we shouldn't get distracted by the crowd on the sidelines. Instead, we should look to Him, for He ran the race with endurance and triumphed. He endured the cross, suffered the shame, and finally crossed the finish line to sit down at the right hand of God the Father.

And what kind of person is this Jesus to whom we are to run? An experienced runner Himself. A runner with perfect form. But most of all, one who is compassionate and sympathetic to our stumblings (Heb. 4:15).

Attitude While Running

A positive attitude is important if a runner is to hang tough and fight off the fatigue and physical pain of the race. Such an attitude is encouraged in chapter 12.

---

6. Brooke Foss Westcott, *The Epistle to the Hebrews* (reprint; Grand Rapids, Mich.: William B. Eerdmans Publishing Co., 1973), pp. 394–95. For a good example of what this verse means see Acts 7:55–56, which describes Stephen in his hour of martyrdom.

For consider Him who has endured such hostility by sinners against Himself, so that you may not grow weary and lose heart. (v. 3)

The word *consider* means "to reckon, compare, weigh, or think over." The salient point is that we are to so fix our eyes on Jesus that our minds block out any distractions. As we meditate on the grueling race He ran, with all its catcalls from the carping crowd, we can't help but feel a burst of adrenaline for the faltering legs of our faith.

You may never win any gold medals, but if you remember the training you've received, if you keep your eyes on the author and perfecter of your faith, oh, you'll run—like a true champion. As the prophet Isaiah said,

> He gives power to the tired and worn out, and strength to the weak. Even the youths shall be exhausted, and the young men will all give up. But they that wait upon the Lord shall renew their strength. They shall mount up with wings like eagles; they shall run and not be weary; they shall walk and not faint. (Isa. 40:29–31 LB)

Living Insights STUDY ONE

In his commentary on Hebrews, F. F. Bruce coaches us with this helpful tip concerning the "encumbrances" that weigh us down, drain our energy, and impede our progress.

> The athlete must discipline himself; he must divest himself of all superfluous weight, not only of heavy objects carried about the body but of excess bodily weight. There are many things which may be perfectly all right in their own way, but which hinder a competitor in the race of faith; they are "weights" which must be laid aside. It may well be that what is a hindrance to one entrant in this spiritual contest is not a hindrance to another; each must learn for himself what in his case is a weight or impediment.[7]

---

7. F. F. Bruce, *The Epistle to the Hebrews* (1964; reprint, Grand Rapids, Mich.: William B. Eerdmans Publishing Co., 1988), p. 349.

As you run with endurance the race that is set before you, are there any encumbrances slowing your spiritual pace? A particular habit, perhaps? Or maybe a lack of mental discipline, an indifferent attitude, procrastination, or impatience? Remember, it's not any particular sin you're looking for, just weights that, if removed, would enable you to run longer, stronger, faster. Think about it, and if you discover one or more, write them down in the space provided.

_____

_____

_____

_____

Starting today, what could you do to divest yourself of the encumbrances you've discovered? Use the following space to describe how—be as specific as possible.

_____

_____

_____

_____

_____

_____

Living Insights   STUDY TWO

The stadium is packed. The excited crowd roars its anticipation as the world-class runners take up their starting positions. But what's this? The runner in lane four is lining up with a portable ten-inch television in his hands. He seems to be watching it instead of keeping his eyes on the race.

Boom! The runners burst out of their blocks—all except the runner in lane four. He's still watching his TV. Wait! Now he's moving. It must be a commercial. Wow, look at him go—and with a TV in his arms, no less! Incredibly, he's starting to gain on the pack. He's passed the last fellow. He's moving into the middle. The crowd can't believe it! He's approaching the lead. Everyone's on their feet. Coming down the final stretch. The fans are going crazy! He's going to do it, he's going to . . . uh-oh—the commercials are over.

Sound ridiculous? Of course it is. Can you imagine actually trying to win a race encumbered with a television?

Some of us may not have to imagine it—we're doing it. Not in the physical realm, but in our spiritual footrace. Watching television is certainly no sin, but for many of us it would definitely classify as an encumbrance to our spiritual growth. Why? Because it simply takes too much of our time. Instead of fixing our eyes on Jesus and competing in the race set before us, we idly sit with our eyes fixed on the television, while afternoons and evenings pass us by.

Is the television slowing you down? Do you need to lay aside a few sitcoms and soap operas so that you can improve your running? If so, try cutting your viewing time in half and see how much time that would free up. Two, maybe three hours? A whole evening? A couple of afternoons? Write down the amount of time you've saved, as well as the time of day.

Monday _____

_____

Tuesday _____

_____

Wednesday _____

_____

Thursday _____

_____

Friday _____

_____

Saturday _____

_____

Now, brainstorm some ways you can use this newly freed-up time to win the imperishable prize of loving God and others as yourself. Like serving meals to the homeless. Joining a Bible study group. Comforting the sick. Repairing the home of a shut-in. Encouraging someone in a letter. Volunteering a few hours each week for a cause you feel passionate about. That's running—and everybody wins (Prov. 11:25).

Chapter 5

Taking a Stand

2 Timothy 4:1–5

Here's a recipe that everyone should know: Frog Legs à la Hoi Polloi.

Take one pot the size of America. Pour in a rich diversity of peoples and cultures. Stir gently. Cook on low heat, gradually raising the temperature by increasing the godlessness in unnoticeable increments for three to four generations, and—voilà! You've got a whole society boiled to death spiritually. Their consciences have been completely seared without one whimper of pain or protest.

The trick, of course, is to increase the immorality so gradually that the people never become aware of the rising danger. In the end, no one takes a stand because they haven't a leg left to stand on!

America is the great melting pot of the world. Within her borders simmers a giant gumbo spiced with every type of seasoning—and it's nearing the boiling point. The heat is dangerously high, and yet, so few are taking a stand. Already, millions of us are inured to the searing presence of abortion, pornography, corruption, injustice, sexual promiscuity, and violence surrounding us. We touch, taste, and handle things today that would've scalded our parents. Yet we say, "It doesn't bother me." And we think that's progress?

Our Times—Difficult and Desperate

For a clearer picture of today's searing moral climate, let's turn to the apostle Paul's prophetic words in 2 Timothy 3.

Stated in Scripture

> But realize this, that in the last days difficult times will come. (v. 1)

"The last days"—when is that? The New Testament writers regarded the period between the first century and Christ's return as the last days. So, to paraphrase Paul, we must realize this: Now that we are in the last days, difficult times have come.

What exactly does Paul mean by "difficult"? Commentator William Barclay explains.

> *Difficult* is the Greek word *chalepos*. It is the normal

Greek word for *difficult*, but it has certain usages which explain its meaning here. It is used in Matthew 8:28 to describe the two Gergesene demoniacs who met Jesus among the tombs. They were violent and dangerous. It is used in Plutarch to describe what we would call an *ugly* wound. It is used by ancient writers on astrology to describe what we would call a *threatening* conjunction of the heavenly bodies. There is the idea of menace and of danger in this word.[1]

Paul depicts an exceedingly violent, savage, fierce time—our time—and then he chronicles the causes that make it so.

For men will be lovers of self, lovers of money, boastful, arrogant, revilers, disobedient to parents, ungrateful, unholy, unloving, irreconcilable, malicious gossips, without self-control, brutal, haters of good, treacherous, reckless, conceited, lovers of pleasure rather than lovers of God; holding to a form of godliness, although they have denied its power; . . . always learning and never able to come to the knowledge of the truth. (vv. 2–5a, 7)

Isn't this what we see illustrated in one form or another in the newspapers and evening news every day?

Illustrated in Life

Not to be melodramatic but just to emphasize the rising immoral temperature of our times, let's consider the film industry. When we compare the depiction of nudity, profanity, and violence that so gratuitously panders to audiences today with what people were watching only two generations ago, there can be no argument against Paul's description of our day.[2]

Here are a few other examples of how things have changed: remember when pornography wasn't splashed all over our magazine racks; when it was safe, even for women, to walk on a street at

1. William Barclay, *The Letters to Timothy, Titus, and Philemon*, rev. ed., The Daily Study Bible Series (Philadelphia, Pa.: Westminster Press, 1975), p. 182.

2. For further study on this topic, see Michael Medved's *Hollywood vs. America: Popular Culture and the War on Traditional Values* (New York, N.Y.: HarperCollins Publishers, Zondervan, 1992).

night; when trusting in God was commended instead of condemned; when marriage vows were upheld and children were valued; when the punishment of the criminal was encouraged; when politicians were, indeed, servants of the people; when our society functioned on a bedrock of biblical absolutes instead of a slippery moral relativism? The melting pot is boiling over with adultery, child abuse, prejudice, crime, drug abuse, poverty, homosexuality, and, as Paul says, "evil men and impostors [who] will proceed from bad to worse, deceiving and being deceived" (v. 13).

Our Stand—Clear and Concise

In light of the difficult times in which we live, how do we as Christians take a stand to endure? What can we do to protect our faith from being ravaged by such troubled waters? Paul provides us with some specific safeguards in the fourth chapter of 2 Timothy.

What We Are to Do

To make sure he has our attention, the Apostle opens this chapter with these sobering words.

> I solemnly charge you in the presence of God and of Christ Jesus, who is to judge the living and the dead, and by His appearing and His kingdom. (2 Tim. 4:1)

In effect, Paul is saying, "I solemnly charge you to listen up!" His tone couldn't be any more serious. And the first instruction for us is this: *Make the Scriptures your standard.*

> Preach the word; be ready in season and out of season; reprove, rebuke, exhort, with great patience and instruction. (v. 2)

In difficult times, like those Paul described in chapter 3, it is easy to drift from the standard of God's Word. Instead of raising our children according to godly principles, we can get swept away by the current of relativistic values embraced in the marketplace. Instead of seeking God's will in His Word, we can flow with the tide of opinion offered by others. Books, friends, and counselors are very helpful at times. But it is the Bible we're to know, to practice, to herald above all else.

Drawing from the phrase "be ready in season and out of season" in verse 2,[3] the second principle to remember is: *Be persistently on the alert.* The Greek term for *ready* means "to be at hand, to have an alert mind." Paul adjures us to keep our minds sharp, honed on the truth of God instead of dulled by the godlessness that surrounds us. Mental discipline is a must if we're to think with discernment in these muddled times.

Tucked away in the commands "reprove, rebuke, exhort, with great patience and instruction" is our third charge from Paul: *Take a stand.* The Apostle admonishes us to confront and, when necessary, to stand alone but not aloof.

While a teenage student at Yale University, the great American theologian Jonathan Edwards wrote in his diary:

> Resolved: that all men should live for the glory of God. Resolved second: that whether others do or not, I will.[4]

That's taking a stand!

Why We Are to Do It

There are many reasons why it is crucial for Christians to take a stand today. Paul mentions two in verses 3–4.

> For the time will come when they will not endure sound doctrine; but wanting to have their ears tickled, they will accumulate for themselves teachers in accordance to their own desires; and will turn away their ears from the truth, and will turn aside to myths.

Note first that the Apostle says the *truth is rejected*—willfully. It's not as if people aren't hearing the truth. They hear it all right. Yet, "they will not endure" it. Why? Because they want to have their "ears tickled" by those who will tell them only what they want to hear, not what God says they need. So they search among the plethora of authors, teachers, counselors, and preachers available today until they find someone with a theology loose enough to accommodate their desires.

---

3. The Amplified Bible sheds light on the phrase "in season and out of season" by rendering it as: "whether the opportunity seems to be favorable or unfavorable, whether it is convenient or inconvenient, whether it is welcome or unwelcome."

4. Jonathan Edwards, as quoted by Marshall Shelley in *Well-Intentioned Dragons* (Waco, Tex.: Word Books Publisher, 1985), p. 49.

Another reason it's important to take a stand is that *lies are supported*. When people reject the truth, they attempt to fill the resulting spiritual vacuum with myths. They not only vigorously pursue falsehood, they also rigorously promote it. Edmund Burke once said,

> All that is necessary for the triumph of evil is that good men do NOTHING![5]

Unless we take a stand, are continually on the alert, and make the Scriptures our standard, the lies supported by those who have rejected the truth will capture the hearts and minds of millions.

How We Are to Do It

Summing up his instructions, Paul leaves us with four concise injunctions that should characterize our efforts in taking a stand.

> But you, be sober in all things, endure hardship, do the work of an evangelist, fulfill your ministry. (v. 5)

First, we're to stand *calmly*. The word *sober* here doesn't refer to the absence of alcohol; rather, it means the absence of a lunatic fanaticism—the kind that belligerently wages war against the lost instead of loving them.

Second, we're to "endure hardship," which means we're to stand *patiently*, even in the midst of mistreatment.

Third, we're to *diligently* "do the work of an evangelist"—a basic requirement of all believers.

Fourth, we're to "fulfill our ministry," meaning that we do it thoroughly. Commit yourself to work heartily as unto the Lord (Col. 3:23–24). Instead of settling for mediocrity, strive for excellence and fulfill all God has given you to do.

Our Impact—Pure and Practical

When we apply Paul's counsel and take a stand in today's difficult times, we can expect certain results:

- Being unique makes an impact.

- Being pure provides a model.

---

5. Edmund Burke, as quoted in *Knight's Master Book of New Illustrations*, comp. Walter B. Knight (Grand Rapids, Mich.: William B. Eerdmans Publishing Co., 1956), p. 430.

- Being consistent keeps us stable.

- Being committed gives us determination.

The next time you're feeling pressured to give up, give in, or get out because the melting pot is too hot, remember these words from Winston Churchill, someone who knew about taking a stand in difficult times:

> Never give in, never give in, never, never, never,
> never—in nothing, great or small, large or petty—
> never give in except to convictions of honor and
> good sense.[6]

Living Insights

Taking a stand is unpopular today. The current consensus of how Christians should exercise their faith can be summed up in one word—*privately*. It's considered egregiously gauche to actually let our beliefs show, much less tell others about them. People take offense at such wanton moral flirtations. How dare we?

But, of course, if we want to promote pornography, or support the slaughter of millions of unborn babies through abortion, or show degenerate "art," or teach children that they're proud descendants of chance + time + primordial slime, then please, by all means, go ahead and take a stand. People will applaud you, and the government will give you money!

This mixed-up moral bigotry evidenced in so many circles today is exactly what Isaiah experienced in his day, when people called evil good, and good evil (Isa. 5:20). And that prejudice is so strong that many Christians have allowed it to browbeat their beliefs into a closet. In the end, their faith becomes so privatized that it is completely ineffectual.

If Paul were here today, he'd probably laugh at such a contradiction as a "private faith." So would his friend James, who wrote,

> For just as the body without the spirit is dead, so
> also faith without works is dead. (James 2:26)

---

6. Winston Churchill, as quoted in *Bartlett's Familiar Quotations*, 15th ed., rev. and enl., ed. Emily Morison Beck (Boston, Mass.: Little, Brown and Co., 1980), p. 745.

The two apostles would scorn the idea that faith has no right to appear in public. Their blood would boil at the way good is being ridiculed as evil. Doesn't yours? Haven't you had enough of the arrogant and the unholy taking a stand to promote evil as being good?

The smell of gunpowder is in Paul's words in 2 Timothy 4. He fires a charge that our faith must be public, not private: We're to stand, not shrink. Fight back, not surrender. By all means be unique and make an impact. Be a model others can follow. Bring whatever areas of your faith may be hiding in a closet out into the open, and be consistent. Make a commitment.

Jesus said,

> "He who is not with Me is against Me; and he who does not gather with Me scatters." (Matt. 12:30)

Are you with Him?

Living Insights   STUDY TWO

The important question for those of us who are willing to take a stand is "How?" How am I going to do this at work, in my neighborhood, at school, in politics, at home, or on the street?

Using the space provided, select three major areas in your life where taking a stand will impact others. Then, applying the four how-to's given in the lesson—calmly, patiently, diligently, and thoroughly—try listing at least three specific ways you can improve your stand for the Lord in each.

Area: _____

1) _____

2) _____

3) _____

Area: _____

1) _____

2) _____

3) _____

Area: _____

1) _____

2) _____

3) _____

Chapter 6

FINISHING A TASK

2 Timothy 4:6–8

Let me ask you something. How many of the Christians you knew back when you first became a believer are still in the running, spiritually speaking?

How many of the committed Christians you knew in high school had dropped the committed part by your ten-year reunion?

How many seventy- or eighty-year-olds do you know who have been believers for decades and are finishing strong in the faith?

Some of you may know several. But many of us can hardly name one. The sad thing is, that's not uncommon. It seems there are plenty who start well in Christianity, but few who end well.

William Barclay writes,

> It is easy to begin but hard to finish. The one thing necessary for life is staying-power, and that is what so many people lack. It was suggested to a certain very famous man that his biography should be written while he was still alive. He absolutely refused to give permission, and his reason was: "I have seen so many men fall out on the last lap."[1]

Why do so many fall out before the race is over? Because of the type of race it is—a lifelong marathon whose course is unpredictable and challenging. Because we're required to run in conditions that are menacing, harsh, and violent. Because we're human—and sometimes we respond to the pressures of the course in the wrong way.

Common Responses to Pressure

As you look around at the ways people commonly react to today's tough times, you'll see three basic responses. First, there's the response of *indifference*: "Relax, don't let things bother you. It'll all work itself out after a while." In his book *World Aflame*, Billy Graham comments on this kind of irresponsible passivity.

---

1. William Barclay, *The Letters to Timothy, Titus, and Philemon*, rev. ed., The Daily Study Bible Series (Philadelphia, Pa.: Westminster Press, 1975), p. 210.

In a declining culture, one of its characteristics is that the ordinary people are unaware of what is happening. Only those who know and can read the signs of decadence are posing the questions that as yet have no answers. Mr. Average Man is comfortable in his complacency and as unconcerned as a silverfish ensconced in a carton of discarded magazines on world affairs. Man is not asking any questions, because his social benefits from the government give him a false security. This is his trouble and his tragedy. Modern man has become a spectator of world events, observing on his television screen without becoming involved. He watches the ominous events of our times pass before his eyes, while he sips his beer in a comfortable chair. He does not seem to realize what is happening to him. He does not understand that his world is on fire and that he is about to be burned with it.[2]

The second response, which is the total opposite of the first, is one of *impulsiveness*: "Do something, even if it's wrong!" Forget trying to get these people to think about consequences; they are only interested in finding immediate relief from the pain of having their faith stretched. Sadly, far too many Christian laypeople and leaders are running for comfortable seats on the sidelines instead of enduring to the finish line.

A third common response is based in *insecurity*: "Watch what others are doing and then do that." Fear has these people looking to conform with the pack rather than racing ahead and setting the pace with Christ.

Biblical Counsel on Determination

- Indifference—results in irresponsibility.

- Impulsiveness—leads to disobedience.

- Insecurity—requires that we conform.

If these are obviously the wrong responses to running in rough times, what, then, are the right choices that will enable us to finish

2. Billy Graham, *World Aflame* (Minneapolis, Minn.: Billy Graham Evangelistic Association, 1965), p. 15.

strong? Let's turn to 2 Timothy 4 and draw four helpful guidelines from the words of someone who finished the course—the apostle Paul.

Face the Facts Realistically

> For I am already being poured out as a drink offering, and the time of my departure has come. (v. 6)

Paul wrote this while locked in a Roman dungeon. The day of his death, perhaps the hour, was close at hand, and he faced that fact squarely. He refused to entertain the unrealistic hope that he might have any more laps left to go as a missionary. To deny the reality of his situation would only weaken his determination. And Paul was determined to stay strong, so he wrote the truth, painful as it was.

To finish well, we, too, must realistically face the facts that cross our paths. Only then will we find ways to hurdle the problems and stay on course. For example, have you taken a marriage vow? Then be realistic about the cost involved to see that bond preserved until the finish. Be realistic about the expectations you put on your spouse. And be realistic about the problems between you; instead of denying them and letting them fester and weaken your commitment, deal with them head-on so they can be resolved.

Be Committed to Finishing What You Start

> I have fought the good fight, I have finished the course, I have kept the faith. (v. 7)

In Greek, the grammar of this sentence is structured to emphasize "the fight," "the course," and "the faith." From these three statements, we can draw out three important ingredients essential to finishing:

- "fought the good fight"—we need to be tough,
- "finished the course"—we need to have a plan, and
- "kept the faith"—we need to walk with God.

First of all, we've got to be tough to finish what we start. It involves fighting against difficult times, grueling circumstances, even ourselves in the sense of battling bad habits and attitudes that slow us down. That's a lot to wage war against, and we won't win unless we've got a firm faith with which to fight.

Second, finishing the course takes a plan. Building up the enduring faith that it takes to finish the course doesn't happen by chance. It's the result of a disciplined pursuit of God. Prayer, Bible study, meditation, worship, and other spiritual exercises must be built into our lives if we are to develop the faith that will carry us to the finish line.

Third, to win we must walk with God, not just talk about Him. We can be tough, have all the right disciplines, and still miss the Lord. Consider the Ephesians Jesus addressed in Revelation 2. He commends them for their deeds, toil, and perseverance, but . . . "I have this against you, that you have left your first love" (v. 4). That first love was Jesus Himself. The Ephesians had become consumed by their job, not their God. Be careful not to let your service for God become a substitute for your relationship with Him.

Focus on the Future When the Present Is Difficult

> In the future there is laid up for me the crown of righteousness, which the Lord, the righteous Judge, will award to me on that day. (2 Tim. 4:8a)

What's Paul doing here? He's looking ahead. Instead of focusing on his immediate execution, he's anticipating the reward he will receive from His beloved Savior for finishing the course. And that thought comforts him in that depressing dungeon, perhaps even puts a smile on his face, a smile his captors cannot understand.

Are you struggling to get through school? Focus on graduating. Picture yourself crossing that stage to receive the hard-earned prize of your diploma. Think about the future benefits of completing your education.

Are you raising a houseful of small people with sticky fingers and dirty diapers? Take your focus off the grape-jelly handprints on your couch and put it on the end product—mature adults who love God and can hand their enduring faith to the next generation.

Whatever your circumstances, encourage yourself by focusing on the finish line. How? Picturing your goal helps, but it's even better to rely on prayer. Concentrate on the hope that you have—God's future handling of your situation.

Realize You Are Not the Only One Standing Firm

> The Lord, the righteous Judge, will award to me on that day; and not only to me, but also to all who

47

have loved His appearing. (v. 8b)

One of the most demoralizing thoughts we can be hit with as we struggle to endure is the idea that we're all alone, that somehow we're strangely different from other believers, that no one else has the same difficulties we do.

Has that happened to you before? You probably felt guilty and ashamed about your shortcomings. And it was those same feelings that kept you from sharing your struggles with anyone else. You figured they'd probably shake their heads in utter horror and say, "You're wrestling with what?" and immediately burn you at the stake. But then you overheard a Christian friend describe his or her trials, and lo and behold, they were the same as yours! Suddenly the terrible weight of feeling like a spiritual pariah was lifted as you realized that your problems are not unique, that you're not alone. We all face similar hurdles as we run the race set before us. Take comfort in that simple fact, and don't let any false ideas about being alone trip you up.

When You Feel like Quitting . . .

In the Bible, even the best of runners went through times when they felt like quitting. Take Elijah, for example. When Queen Jezebel threatened his life after his victory on Mount Carmel,

> he was afraid and arose and ran for his life and came
> to Beersheba, which belongs to Judah, and left his
> servant there. But he himself went a day's journey
> into the wilderness, and came and sat down under
> a juniper tree; and he requested for himself that he
> might die, and said, "It is enough; now, O Lord, take
> my life, for I am not better than my fathers."
> (1 Kings 19:3–4)

Moses went through a similar time as he led the children of Israel in the wilderness (Num. 11:10–15), and we can be sure that we will too. The temptation to quit is common to us all. So what can we do to keep from giving up? First, we can *count our blessings.* More than just an empty cliché, this simple exercise can marshal forth great reserves of encouraging memories that will add strength to our stride. Take a moment to reflect on God's past faithfulness, and you'll find the faith to trust Him for the future.

Second, *remind yourself that whatever is worth having is worth sacrificing for.* Is finishing strong worth the sacrifice? Jesus thought so . . . remember?

> Jesus, the author and perfecter of faith, who for the joy set before Him endured the cross, despising the shame, and has sat down at the right hand of the throne of God. (Heb. 12:2)

Finishing well takes great sacrifice—but it promises even greater rewards. Keep running!

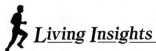 *Living Insights* STUDY ONE

Years ago, Admiral Hyman Rickover was the head of the United States Nuclear Navy and personally interviewed and approved every officer aboard a nuclear submarine. Among those he interviewed was former president Jimmy Carter. Here is Carter's account of that unforgettable interview.

> It was the first time I met Admiral Rickover, and we sat in a large room by ourselves for more than two hours, and he let me choose any subjects I wished to discuss. Very carefully, I chose those about which I knew most at the time—current events, seamanship, music, literature, naval tactics, electronics, gunnery—and he began to ask me a series of questions of increasing difficulty. In each instance, he soon proved that I knew relatively little about the subject I had chosen.
>
> He always looked right into my eyes, and he never smiled. I was saturated with cold sweat.
>
> Finally, he asked a question and I thought I could redeem myself. He said, "How did you stand in your class at the Naval Academy?" Since I had completed my sophomore year at Georgia Tech before entering Annapolis as a plebe, I had done very well, and I swelled my chest with pride and answered, "Sir, I stood fifty-ninth in a class of 820!" I sat back to wait for the congratulations—which never came. Instead, the question: "Did you do your best?" I started to say, "Yes, sir," but I remembered who this was and

recalled several of the many times at the Academy when I could have learned more about our allies, our enemies, weapons, strategy, and so forth. I was just human. I finally gulped and said, "No, sir, I didn't always do my best."

He looked at me for a long time, and then turned his chair around to end the interview. He asked one final question, which I have never been able to forget—or to answer. He said, "Why not?" I sat there for a while, shaken, and then slowly left the room.[3]

Powerful story—and point. Suppose for a moment that you were the one being interviewed by Admiral Rickover. This time, however, the topic isn't about running nuclear submarines for America, but running a spiritual race for Christ, your race, and here's the question: "Are you doing your best to finish well?"

This is the part where ex-president Carter got nuked. You're probably feeling torpedoed too. Few, if any, survive a direct hit like that question . . . which raises Rickover's final bombshell. You know what to ask yourself. Think about it—could it be that you're responding to today's pressures in any of the three ways described in our study? Use the space provided to log your thoughts.

_____

_____

_____

_____

_____

_____

Living Insights

Instead of looking years ahead to when we might die and speculating on whether we'll end strong, let's ask ourselves how well we're finishing now in the shorter, less glamorous dashes of life.

3. As quoted by Gordon MacDonald in *Ordering Your Private World*, exp. ed. (Nashville, Tenn.: Thomas Nelson Publishers, Oliver-Nelson, 1985), pp. 94–95.

Take, for example, that children's Sunday school class you agreed to teach for a couple of months. Are you doing your best to pray and prepare each week, or are you winging it? How about that project you're working on for your boss? Will the finished product be first-class, or simply mediocre? And what about when you're called to do some behind-the-scenes work? Do you stay at it until it's done right, or do you settle for "good enough to get by"?

Poet Ruth Harms Calkin contemplates this same question in a beautiful poem titled "I Wonder."

You know, Lord, how I serve You
With great emotional fervor
In the limelight.
You know how eagerly I speak for You
At a women's club.
You know how I effervesce when I promote
A fellowship group.
You know my genuine enthusiasm
At a Bible study.

But how would I react, I wonder
If You pointed to a basin of water
And asked me to wash the calloused feet
Of a bent and wrinkled old woman
Day after day
Month after month
In a room where nobody saw
And nobody knew.[4]

Do you really want to know how well you're going to finish in the future? Then look at how you are finishing in the short dashes today.

4. "I Wonder" by Ruth Harms Calkin, *Tell Me Again Lord, I Forget* (Wheaton, Ill.: Tyndale House Publishers, 1974), p. 23.

Chapter 7

DEALING WITH OPPOSITION
2 Timothy 4:9–10, 14–18

Away with him! Blasphemous traitor! Infidel!"

The violent mob dragged the apostle Paul out of the temple and began kicking and stomping and hitting him in a furious rage of unhinged fanatical fervor.

"Son of a devil! Demon! Don't let the heretic live!"

And they almost didn't. Had it not been for the Roman soldiers who intervened, Paul surely would have been killed (see Acts 21). This is but one example of the opposition the Apostle faced. From the start of his conversion to the finish line of his execution, the hurdles of opposition placed in Paul's path were constant and cruel: heckled, rejected, cursed, hunted like prey, abandoned, beaten with rods, whipped, stoned, lied about, ridiculed, hounded, arrested, and imprisoned. Yet despite all these, he finished faithfully. He endured to the end.

It was near the finish line, in view of the executioner's axe, that the Apostle penned his second and final letter to Timothy. And in the closing of that letter and life, he gives us a glimpse of two men who opposed him, two who made his life even harder.

Identifying the Resistance

It is important to understand the identity of this letter's recipient. Timothy was Paul's spiritual protégé. More than that, he had become one of the Apostle's closest companions. Together they had traveled extensively as missionaries, faced many dangers, and helped each other overcome numerous obstacles. Still, there were two hurdles the experienced Apostle felt he should forewarn the young pastor about.

By Name

> Make every effort to come to me soon; for De-mas, having loved this present world, has deserted me and gone to Thessalonica. (2 Tim. 4:9–10a)

Others had forsaken Paul before (v. 16), but here he names one deserter in particular—Demas.

The second name Paul points out is that of an adversary— someone who deliberately set out to destroy the Apostle and his ministry.

Alexander the coppersmith did me much harm; the Lord will repay him according to his deeds. Be on guard against him yourself, for he vigorously opposed our teaching. (vv. 14–15)

Demas and Alexander—they represent the opposite ends in the spectrum of opposition. Let's take a closer look at their contrasting methods as revealed in Paul's words to Timothy.

By Method

Demas' method of opposition is what you might call passive disagreement—he deserted Paul. The Greek term for *desert* means "to abandon, to leave in the lurch, to let down." Besides leaving the Apostle physically, Demas deserted Paul in a time of crisis, when he really needed him.

What caused this once-faithful friend to abandon the Apostle? Paul explains it all with that one short but damning phrase: "having loved this present world" (v. 10). The Greek rendition of this is even more descriptive: "having loved the now age." What exactly is the "now age"? Bishop Trench calls it

> that mass of thoughts, opinions, maxims, specula-
> tions, hopes, impulses, aims, aspirations, at any time
> current in the world, which it may be impossible to
> seize and accurately define, but which constitute a
> most real and effective power, being the moral, or
> immoral, atmosphere which at every moment of our
> lives we inhale, again inevitably to exhale.[1]

Demas had inhaled deeply, and it left him intoxicated with the pleasures of the world rather than with the Lord. How did it happen? No one really knows for sure. However, William Barclay traces a possibility that is all too probable—one we would do well to note.

---

1. Richard Chenevix Trench, as quoted by Homer A. Kent, Jr. in *The Pastoral Epistles* (Chicago, Ill.: Moody Press, 1982), pp. 289–90.

There are three mentions of [Demas] in Paul's letters; and it may well be that they have in them the story of a tragedy. In Philemon 24 he is listed amongst a group of men whom Paul calls his *fellow-labourers*. In Colossians 4:14 he is mentioned without any comment at all. Here he has forsaken Paul because he loved this present world. First, Demas the fellow-labourer, then, just Demas, and, finally, Demas the deserter who loved the world. Here is the history of a spiritual degeneration. Bit by bit the fellow-labourer has become the deserter; the title of honour has become the name of shame.[2]

In contrast to Demas' opposition, which was to passively walk away, Alexander's aggressive assault attacked both Paul's person and his teaching.

The first form of assault is referred to in the phrase "did me much harm" (v. 14). That little word *did* in Greek is *endeiknumi*, from which we get the word *indictment*. It means "to show forth, display, to point out," and it was often used in Paul's day for pointing out information against a person. That's what Alexander was doing, with a vengeance, to Paul. No doubt, he concocted half-truths about the Apostle's character and background that Paul says did him much harm.

Alexander also "vigorously opposed" Paul's teaching (v. 15). He actively assaulted the truth being preached. He wasn't satisfied to simply reject the gospel personally; he felt it necessary to undertake a zealous crusade against the message.

Handling the Opposition

If there's one truth we could glean from Paul's life thus far, it's that we cannot expect to make an impact for Christ without opposition. Whether it's the passive defection of a Demas, an aggressive assault of an Alexander, or something in between, opposition will come, and we must train ourselves to be able to overcome it. How? What should we do? Again, if we look closely at Paul's comments concerning Demas and Alexander, we can pick up three important principles that Paul practiced.

2. William Barclay, *The Letters to Timothy, Titus, and Philemon*, rev. ed., The Daily Study Bible Series (Philadelphia, Pa.: Westminster Press, 1975), pp. 212–13.

Realistically

First, notice that in both cases Paul names his opposers and candidly states the facts about them. He's direct, unafraid, and realistic about what has happened and the damage that's been done. It would be easier and less unpleasant to ignore such painful events, to make excuses for such people, but the Apostle chooses to state the truth rather than dodge it.

Positively

Second, observe how positively Paul handles the opposition. In verse 16 he says:

> At my first defense no one supported me, but all deserted me [just like Demas]; may it not be counted against them.

"May it not be counted against them." Isn't that an incredible statement of grace and compassion? Just when you might expect Paul to say something bitter toward Demas or the others who deserted him, he comes out with a beautiful statement reminiscent of Jesus' merciful loving-kindness on the cross, "Father, forgive them; for they do not know what they are doing" (Luke 23:34).

As for Alexander, Paul says, "The Lord will repay him according to his deeds" (2 Tim. 4:14b). Rather than striking back on his own, the Apostle trusts the Lord to handle his opposition. That's the right response to being wronged. And no one should know this better than Paul, who wrote,

> Never pay back evil for evil to anyone. Respect what is right in the sight of all men. If possible, so far as it depends on you, be at peace with all men. Never take your own revenge, beloved, but leave room for the wrath of God, for it is written, "Vengeance is Mine, I will repay," says the Lord. (Rom. 12:17–19)

By keeping his focus on his holy and righteous God, who will one day exact a terrible punishment on the Alexanders of this world, Paul was able to restrain the natural temptation to seek his own revenge.[3]

---

3. That Paul was keeping his focus on the Lord is evident from the text: verse 14—"The Lord will repay him"; verse 17—"The Lord stood with me"; verse 18—"The Lord will deliver me."

Firmly

The third principle tucked away in Paul's writing is a crucial one. Many believers have the mistaken idea that, just because God tells us not to take revenge, we're to be submissive doormats for our antagonists to wipe their feet on. Wrong! Look at how firmly the Apostle cautions Timothy to beware of Alexander.

> Be on guard against him yourself. (2 Tim. 4:15a)

Leaving vengeance in the Lord's hands does not mean we let down our guard. We're to exercise wisdom and prudence so as not to give our enemies opportunities to do us harm. If they succeed in attacking us, however, then we're to exercise the positive response of trusting in God's justice instead of implementing our own.

Claiming the Deliverance

Amidst all the desertions and attacks, one encouraging truth about Paul's experience stands out: he was never alone. Jesus always stood by his side.

Claim the Lord's Strength for Today

> But the Lord stood with me, and strengthened me,
> in order that through me the proclamation might
> be fully accomplished, and that all the Gentiles
> might hear; and I was delivered out of the lion's
> mouth. (v. 17)

Just as Christ stood by Paul, He will stand by you and me, offering strength to accomplish His will despite the opposition. Yet we may refuse His help, as many do, because our eyes are often overwhelmed by the size of our enemy instead of our God. As G. K. Chesterton once said,

> [Christianity] has not been tried and found wanting;
> it has been found difficult and left untried.[4]

As Christians living in a fallen world, we can be sure that each day will marshal forth new opposition to living for Christ. Therefore, we must train ourselves to claim Christ's strength, without

---

4. G. K. Chesterton, as quoted in *Bartlett's Familiar Quotations*, 15th ed., rev. and enl., ed. Emily Morison Beck (Boston, Mass.: Little, Brown and Co., 1980), p. 742.

reservation, in every battle. Our faith cannot withstand attack without His reinforcement.

Commit Every Future Event into His Hands

Another encouraging truth that kept Paul going forward in the midst of opposition was his assurance about the future.

> The Lord will deliver me from every evil deed, and will bring me safely to His heavenly kingdom; to Him be the glory forever and ever. Amen. (v. 18)

Oftentimes, the number-one opponent to walking by faith is fear: fear of further evil deeds and fear concerning our ultimate safety in His kingdom. Paul overcame both with a victorious faith that committed every future event into God's hands. And He is willing to help us overcome our fears too, if we will but place our future in His hands.

Conclusion

Have you ever been deserted by a Demas in a time of crisis? Is there an Alexander in your life, whose sole mission is to misunderstand, misinterpret, and misrepresent you and your teaching? You're not alone. Paul has been there—and Jesus is there by your side. The Lord has taken a stand with you, as Paul says so beautifully in Romans 8:31: "If God is for us, who is against us?"

However large or small, passive or aggressive the opposition that comes your way, never forget who stands with you. Never forget who is eager and able to strengthen you. Never forget who is for you . . .

Jesus.

Living Insights

Opposition often makes us fearful. And, as Maurice Wagner points out in his book *The Sensation of Being Somebody*, fear can become an effective ally for our enemy.

> Fear paralyzes the mind, making us unable to think clearly. Fear of great magnitude disorganizes the mind temporarily so that confusion reigns. Fear also has a way of multiplying itself; we are so disabled

when afraid that we become afraid of our fears. We cannot face problems when we are afraid of them.[5]

Are you feeling fearful about some opposition right now? Perhaps from another Christian attempting to undermine your leadership? Or from a family member who opposes your following Christ? Or maybe from a professor who enjoys attacking Christians in his or her classroom? If so, take hold of these helpful words from Wagner.

> It takes faith to master a fear problem. It is impossible to overcome fear by feeling guilty for the emotion. Nowhere in the Bible does God condemn a person for being afraid; instead He consistently encourages the fearful with such statements as, "Fear thou not; for I am with thee" (Isa. 41:10). When we are afraid, we feel all alone with our problem, and we feel overwhelmed. . . .
>
> . . . When we are obsessed with feelings of such aloneness and unworthiness, it is good to turn to James 4:8 and obey God's invitation: "Draw nigh to God, and he will draw nigh to you." . . . David said, "I sought the Lord, and he heard me, and delivered me from all my fears" (Ps. 34:4).[6]

Fear may have your heart and mind on the run. But you can end the retreat, clear the confusion, and turn this battle around if you will obey God's instructions to draw nigh just as David did in his moment of crisis.

Could you set aside some time to do that today?

Here are a few Scripture passages that will help prepare and guide your heart in seeking the Lord: Psalms 27, 69, 70; Romans 8:31–39; Hebrews 13:5b–6; and 1 Peter 3:13–14.

🏃 Living Insights STUDY TWO

Now that perhaps you've been able to replace your paralyzing fear with a clearheaded faith, you can start addressing the problem of the opposition against you, using the three principles Paul applied.

---

5. Maurice E. Wagner, *The Sensation of Being Somebody* (Grand Rapids, Mich.: Zondervan Publishing House, 1975), p. 190.

6. Wagner, *The Sensation of Being Somebody*, pp. 190–91.

First, *be realistic:* Your first step is to identify the specific person or persons opposing you and the methods they are using. Be sure you have the facts straight before you put any names down.

Second, *be positive:* In light of your particular situation, what would be a positive biblical response? What specific Scriptures support your decision? Here are a few passages you might find helpful in seeking the right response: Matthew 5:43–48; Romans 12:17–21; 1 Peter 3:8–17.

Third, *be firm:* Paul told Timothy to be on guard against Alexander. In what practical ways can you guard yourself against your adversary? See Proverbs 22:3.

Finally, before you act on any of these plans, ask a trusted mentor or friend to evaluate your ideas and make any suggestions.

Chapter 8

LIVING WITH LONELINESS

2 Timothy 4:9–21

*L*oneliness. Few emotions are more painful than the consuming anguish contained in this companionless word. Think of the single person enduring the pain of a broken romance, of the isolated inmate behind steel bars, of the military person stationed overseas, of the widow whose table for two is set for one, or of the young couple whose empty arms ache for the child cancer claimed for its own. These individuals understand the pain of loneliness at a deep and tortuous level.

At times, the race of enduring faith will take all of us down that desolate stretch of track called loneliness. There we will hear no encouraging cheers, feel no encouraging presence—only the burning, forced breaths it takes to keep running, keep believing.

Second Timothy 4 records just such a time in Paul's life. To find him, we must descend a winding stone staircase into the torchlit bowels of Rome's Mamertine prison. The air is damp and chill as we wend our way to a miserably cramped cell secluded in darkness. There we find the great Apostle, the great missionary, the great discipler of God's church—shackled and alone. He's on the home-stretch of his life, and it looks to be loneliness all the way.

When Loneliness Strikes

Loneliness can strike at almost any time and in any place. And even though few of us will ever be struck by it as Paul was—locked inside a dungeon—his parting words bring to mind four other occasions where the chances are high we'll be hit.

When We Are Distant from Cherished Friends

> Make every effort to come to me soon; . . .
> Crescens has gone to Galatia, Titus to Dalmatia.
> . . . Tychicus I have sent to Ephesus. . . .
> Greet Prisca and Aquila, and the household of
> Onesiphorus. Erastus remained at Corinth, but Tro-
> phimus I left sick at Miletus. (vv. 9, 10b, 12, 19–20)

The Apostle doesn't come right out and say he's lonely, but you know he's got to be feeling that way as he writes about all those who have left as well as those he wishes he could see. Will he ever see any of them again? He tries not to dwell on the answer because it only feeds his sense of separation. Outside of the faithful Dr. Luke, no one is left (v. 11). Everyone's gone. And that's the kind of isolation where loneliness thrives.

When Our Memories Bring Nostalgic Reminders

> At my first defense no one supported me, but all deserted me; may it not be counted against them. But the Lord stood with me, and strengthened me, in order that through me the proclamation might be fully accomplished, and that all the Gentiles might hear; and I was delivered out of the lion's mouth. (vv. 16–17)

A bitter memory suddenly prompts the nostalgic reminder of God's goodness—"But the Lord stood with me." It's a "those were the days" moment as the Apostle relives how God strengthened him as only He can. Nostalgic memories are wonderful, but to those caught in the throes of difficult times, they can have the bittersweet effect of magnifying lonely feelings. Paul awakes from his reverie to the fetid smells and hopeless groanings of condemned men— and loneliness is there waiting for him.

When Certain Times of the Year Occur

> Make every effort to come before winter. (v. 21a)

Why winter? Was it because the Apostle felt his death would soon follow nature's own? Or was it simply because there was something about winter that triggered an ineluctable lonesomeness in him? It's a well-known fact that certain times of the year affect people differently. Christmas, for example, is usually a time of joy and celebration, but for those shackled by loneliness, it can be a season of sorrow and despair.

"Come before winter, Timothy. Come warm my heart with your companionship. I need that."

When We Feel Forgotten and Shelved

Everyone experiences loneliness in this way at some time or another, especially those who have once known the joy of being involved and useful but have had it snatched away overnight or

61

siphoned off over a period of time. It can happen so easily—a debilitating sickness, an unexpected change—and suddenly you've been set aside, left behind, or, perhaps even worse, forgotten.

Read between the lines of Paul's last words to Timothy in chapter 4, and there can be no doubt that this was a time in which Paul was vulnerable to feeling forgotten as he sat shelved away deep inside a Roman prison.

What Loneliness Does

Fortunately, loneliness can do more than make us feel miserable. It also works as a catalyst, bringing about some positive changes, two of which are reflected in Paul's comments to Timothy.

Makes Us Aware of Others' Significance

Pick up Mark and bring him with you, for he is useful to me for service. (v. 11b)

There was a time when Paul wouldn't have given a plugged nickel for Mark. Why? Because he had signed on to minister with Paul on his first missionary journey but then later deserted him and returned home (Acts 13:5, 13). It was a bitter experience for Paul, and when Barnabas later suggested they take Mark on their second missionary trip, Paul adamantly refused (15:36–40).

So what did Mark do that eventually changed Paul's mind about him? No one knows for certain, but commentator William Barclay offers this historical insight.

> Tradition has it that he went to Egypt and that he was the founder of the Christian Church in that country. But, whatever he did, he certainly redeemed himself. When Paul comes to write Colossians from his Roman prison, Mark is with him, and Paul commends him to the Colossian Church and charges them to receive him. And now, when the end is near, the one man Paul wants, besides his beloved Timothy, is Mark, for he is a useful man to have about. The quitter has become the man who can turn his hand to anything in the service of Paul and of the gospel.[1]

1. William Barclay, *The Letters to Timothy, Titus, and Philemon*, rev. ed., The Daily Study Bible Series (Philadelphia, Pa.: Westminster Press, 1975), p. 218.

It's a powerful testimony to Mark that Paul asks for him above all the others he could have named. All the more so considering Paul's circumstances—alone, condemned, and likely to put anyone who visits him in danger of being arrested as well. But in his loneliness, he had ample time to reflect on who would be brave enough and committed enough to come to him in his hour of need. And he chose Mark.

Forces Us to Turn Our Concerns Over to God

Something else loneliness does is bring us to a point of dependence on the Lord. Look again at Paul's words. When he felt wronged, whom did he trust to put things right?

> Alexander the coppersmith did me much harm; the Lord will repay him according to his deeds.
> (2 Tim. 4:14)

When he was worried, whom did he trust to deliver him?

> The Lord will deliver me from every evil deed. (v. 18a)

When he was uncertain, who was it that made him safe?

> [The Lord] will bring me safely to His heavenly kingdom; to Him be the glory forever and ever. Amen.
> (v. 18b)

The same feeling of aloneness that isolates us and makes us feel insignificant can also powerfully motivate us to seek the Lord. It can reawaken us to the simple practice we tend to forget in all our busyness—seeking Him one day at a time.

How Loneliness Is Controlled

It would be nice if we could rid ourselves of loneliness once and for all, but none of us can. At best, we can control it by applying the kinds of methods Paul practiced. For example, *investing time with intimate friends*. A person can feel lonely even in the midst of a crowd. It isn't the number of people that helps assuage feelings of loneliness, it's the quality of the relationships that matters. Remember that Paul sought to surround himself with three *intimate* friends: Luke, Timothy, and Mark. These were the men he could connect with, confide in, and be comforted by so that his loneliness would be lifted.

Another important approach to controlling loneliness is *taking care of bodily needs*. Lonely people tend to let themselves go by ceasing to care about their looks, their hygiene, and their diet. Paul didn't, however. Notice his request in verse 13.

> When you come bring the cloak which I left at Troas
> with Carpus.

Even in this small request, the Apostle is clearly taking what precautions he can to protect his health against the chill of that dungeon and the oncoming winter months. To let himself go would only invite sickness of the body and of the mind.

A third way to control loneliness is by *stretching the mind with good books*. Paul asked Timothy not only for his cloak but also for some books (v. 13b). Don't allow loneliness to isolate your thoughts. Instead, stimulate your thinking with good books. Soak up the insights of those who are wise. Let your imagination be stretched, your heart moved, and your mind challenged through the fellowship of great literature available in any library. Reading will not only keep you from withdrawing further into loneliness, it will help pull you out of it altogether.

The final method is *spending time in the Scriptures*. Commenting on Paul's request for "the books, especially the parchments" (v. 13b), William Barclay explains:

> He wants the *books*; the word is *biblia*, which literally means papyrus rolls; and it may well be that these rolls contained the earliest forms of the gospels. He wanted the *parchments*. They could be one of two things. They might be Paul's necessary legal documents, especially his certificate of Roman citizenship; but more likely they were copies of the Hebrew Scriptures, for the Hebrews wrote their sacred books on parchment made from the skins of animals. It was the word of Jesus and the word of God that Paul wanted most of all, when he lay in prison awaiting death.
>
> Sometimes history has a strange way of repeating itself. Fifteen hundred years later William Tyndale was lying in prison in Vilvorde, waiting for death because he had dared to give the people the Bible in their own language. It is a cold damp winter, and

he writes to a friend: "Send me, for Jesus's sake, a warmer cap, something to patch my leggings, a woollen shirt, and *above all my Hebrew Bible*." When they were up against it and the chill breath of death was on them, the great ones wanted more than anything else the word of God to put strength and courage into their souls.[2]

Let history repeat itself again. The next time you're up against loneliness, spend time in the Scriptures, and let God put strength and courage into your soul.

> The Lord be with your spirit. Grace be with you. (v. 22)

Living Insights   STUDY ONE

Everyone goes through times when feelings of loneliness rage out of control. But we needn't wait for those times to hit before we apply the four practical tips gained from Paul for controlling loneliness. They are just as potent when used as preventive, rather than remedial, measures.

In this Living Insight, give yourself a loneliness checkup using the four methods from our lesson.

First: *Investing time with intimate friends.* Do you have two or three intimate friends in whom you can confide, as Paul had with Luke, Timothy, and Mark?

Doing Poorly ❏—❏—❏—❏—❏ Very Healthy

Second: *Taking care of bodily needs.* Are you exercising consistently? Keeping yourself neat and clean? Eating well?

Doing Poorly ❏—❏—❏—❏—❏ Very Healthy

Third: *Stretching your mind with good books.* Are you reading regularly? Are you enjoying a novel or autobiography? Or perhaps something about history, art, or current events?

Doing Poorly ❏—❏—❏—❏—❏ Very Healthy

---

2. Barclay, *The Letters to Timothy, Titus, and Philemon,* pp. 219–20.

Fourth: *Spending time in the Scriptures.* How often and for how long are you studying, meditating, and memorizing the Scriptures?

Doing Poorly ❑——❑——❑——❑——❑ Very Healthy

Based on your findings, what would you prescribe to move the level of your health up at least one notch in those areas where you're doing poorly?

Prescription

_____

_____

_____

_____

_____

🏃 *Living Insights* STUDY TWO

Congratulations, you've made it to the finish line of our study on enduring faith. It's our hope that the coaching and encouragement you've received along the way will enable you to run with greater strength and perseverance the race set before you as a believer.

To cool down after such a hard workout, walk through the following section and write down the particular truths and encouragements from each chapter that have been most helpful to you.

How to Stop Shrinking_____

_____

Profile of a Faith That Endures_____

_____

Looking Back: They Pleased God_____

_____

Living Today: You Can Too!_____

_____

Taking a Stand _____

Finishing a Task _____

Dealing with Opposition _____

Living with Loneliness _____

BOOKS FOR PROBING FURTHER

For those of you who want to continue your training in enduring faith, we recommend these excellent coaches.

Chapell, Bryan. *Standing Your Ground*. Grand Rapids, Mich.: Baker Book House, 1989. Drawing from Daniel's courageous stand during his Babylonian captivity, Bryan Chapell offers messages of comfort and courage to those taking a stand for God today.

Colson, Charles, with Ellen Santilli Vaughn. *Against the Night*. Ann Arbor, Mich.: Servant Publications, Vine Books, 1989. Chuck Colson, a courageous prophet for our day, warns of the encroaching darkness of the times and challenges Christians to renew their commitment to shine as God's lights in the world.

————, with Ellen Santilli Vaughn. *Kingdoms in Conflict*. New York, N.Y.: William Morrow; Grand Rapids, Mich.: Zondervan Publishing House, 1987. Drawing upon his political experience, Colson tackles the barbed issues that confront every Christian wanting to make a stand, especially in a society known for its widespread skirmishes between the kingdoms of church and state.

————. *Who Speaks for God?* Westchester, Ill.: Good News Publishers, Crossway Books, 1985. Within this collection of essays, Colson inspires the church to speak out bravely on Christ's behalf concerning issues in which the world is denying His lordship.

Dravecky, Dave and Jan, with Ken Gire. *When You Can't Come Back*. Grand Rapids, Mich.: Zondervan Publishing House, 1992. Speaking to readers like two close friends, Dave and Jan Dravecky share their struggle to endure in the tough times surrounding the amputation of Dave's cancerous pitching arm. A warm, insightful book that will bring hope and encouragement to everyone facing tough times.

Gire, Ken. *Intimate Moments with the Savior*. Grand Rapids, Mich.: Zondervan Publishing House, 1989. While running the spiritual race, it is easy to sprint right by the very author and perfecter of our faith—Jesus Christ. With superb writing and refreshing insights, Ken Gire slows us down with devotional respites that allow us to cultivate intimate moments with our Savior.

———. *Incredible Moments with the Savior*. Grand Rapids, Mich.: Zondervan Publishing House, 1990. Again Gire pulls us aside to witness Christ's deity and compassion. His compelling style, though, makes us more than mere spectators; we come away from these times inspired by Christ's example to look beyond our needs to the needs of others.

———. *Instructive Moments with the Savior*. Grand Rapids, Mich.: Zondervan Publishing House, 1992. This third of what will be the four-volume devotional masterpiece *Moments with the Savior* strengthens your faith to endure as you learn to hear the Savior through poignant meditations on His parables.

Peterson, Eugene H. *A Long Obedience in the Same Direction*. Downers Grove, Ill.: InterVarsity Press, 1980. Using the Songs of Ascents (Pss. 120–34) the Hebrew pilgrims sang on the their way to worship in Jerusalem, Peterson offers the modern-day pilgrim encouragement to persevere in the lifelong journey of faith.

Whitney, Donald S. *Spiritual Disciplines for the Christian Life*. Colorado Springs, Colo.: NavPress, 1991. Donald Whitney has written an invaluable book for us all on the training of our spiritual disciplines—the very disciplines that will allow God to strengthen our faith to endure to the finish line.

Some of the books listed here may be out of print and available only through a library. All of these works are recommended reading only. With the exception of books by Charles R. Swindoll, none of them are available through Insight for Living. If you wish to obtain some of these suggested readings, please contact your local Christian bookstore.

ACKNOWLEDGMENTS

Insight for Living is grateful to the source below for permission to use their material.

Calkin, Ruth Harms. *Tell Me Again Lord, I Forget*. Wheaton, Ill.: Tyndale House Publishers, 1974. Used by permission of Tyndale House Publishers, Inc. All rights reserved.

NOTES

NOTES

NOTES

ORDERING INFORMATION

Cassette Tapes and Study Guide

This Bible study guide was designed to be used independently or in conjunction with the broadcast of Chuck Swindoll's taped messages on the topic listed below. If you would like to order cassette tapes or further copies of this study guide, please see the information given below and the Order Forms provided at the end of this guide.

FAITH THAT ENDURES . . . IN TIMES LIKE THESE

All around us, Christians of every age and occupation are dropping out of the race set before them as followers of Christ. Often, these individuals explode out of their conversions at full speed, only to tire quickly. Praying becomes labored, Bible study becomes a strain, and many grow weary of life's relentless hurdles. Inevitably, their faith falters and they stumble and fall.

Faith That Endures . . . in Times like These is a study designed to help train your faith to win. But it's not about speed. It's about endurance, obedience, staying faithful to the finish. That's winning faith. And is your faith strong enough to go the distance?

Whether you've just begun the race or are completing your twentieth year as a Christian, these eight chapters of biblical coaching and encouragement will help firm up your faith to press on—all the way to the finish line.

			Calif.*	U.S.	B.C.*	Canada*
FET	CS	Cassette series, includes album cover	$31.32	$29.20	$36.60	$34.20
FET	1–4	Individual cassettes, includes messages A and B	6.76	6.30	7.61	7.23
FET	SG	Study guide	4.26	3.95	5.08	5.08

*These prices already include the following charges: for delivery in **California**, applicable sales tax; **Canada**, 7% GST and 7% postage and handling (on tapes only); **British Columbia**, 7% GST, 6% British Columbia sales tax (on tapes only), and 7% postage and handling (on tapes only). **The prices are subject to change without notice.**

FET   1-A: *How to Stop Shrinking*—Hebrews 10:32–39
        B: *Profile of a Faith That Endures*—Hebrews 11:1–6

FET   2-A: *Looking Back: They Pleased God*—Hebrews 11:6–40
        B: *Living Today: You Can Too!*—Hebrews 12:1–3

FET   3-A: *Taking a Stand*—2 Timothy 4:1–5
        B: *Finishing a Task*— 2 Timothy 4:6–8

FET   4-A: *Dealing with Opposition*—2 Timothy 4:9–10, 14–18
        B: *Living with Loneliness*—2 Timothy 4:9–21

How to Order by Mail

Simply mark on the order form whether you want the series or individual tapes. Mail the form with your payment to the appropriate address listed below. We will process your order as promptly as we can.

United States: Mail your order to the Ordering Services Department at Insight for Living, Post Office Box 69000, Anaheim, California 92817-0900. If you wish your order to be shipped first-class for faster delivery, add 10 percent of the total order amount. Otherwise, please allow four to six weeks for delivery by fourth-class mail. We accept payment by personal check, money order, or credit card. Unfortunately, we are unable to offer invoicing or COD orders.

Canada: Mail your order to Insight for Living Ministries, Post Office Box 2510, Vancouver, British Columbia V6B 3W7. Allow approximately four weeks for delivery. We accept payment by personal check, money order, or credit card. Unfortunately, we are unable to offer invoicing or COD orders.

Australia, New Zealand, or Papua New Guinea: Mail your order to Insight for Living, Inc., GPO Box 2823 EE, Melbourne, Victoria 3001, Australia. Please allow six to ten weeks for delivery by surface mail. If you would like your order sent airmail, the delivery time may be reduced. Using the United States price as a base, add postage costs—surface or airmail— to the amount of your order. Please use the chart that follows to determine correct postage. Due to fluctuating currency rates, we can accept only personal checks made payable in United States funds, international money orders, or credit cards in payment for materials.

Overseas: Other overseas residents should mail their orders to our United States office. Please allow six to ten weeks for delivery by surface mail. If you would like your order sent airmail, the delivery time may be reduced. Using the United States price as a base, add postage costs— surface or airmail—to the amount of your order. Please use the chart that follows to determine correct postage. Due to fluctuating currency rates, we can accept only personal checks made payable in United States funds, international money orders, or credit cards in payment for materials.

Type of Postage	Postage Cost
Surface	10% of total order
Airmail	25% of total order

For Faster Service, Order by Telephone or FAX

For credit card orders, you are welcome to use one of our toll-free numbers between the hours of 7:00 A.M. and 4:30 P.M., Pacific time, Monday through Friday, or our FAX numbers. The numbers to use from anywhere in the United States are **1-800-772-8888** or FAX (714) 575-5049. To order from Canada, call our Vancouver office using **1-800-663-7639** or FAX (604) 596-2975. Vancouver residents, call (604) 596-2910. Australian residents should phone (03) 872-4606. From other international locations, call our Ordering Services Department at (714) 575-5000 in the United States.

Our Guarantee

Our cassettes are guaranteed for ninety days against faulty performance or breakage due to a defect in the tape. For best results, please be sure your tape recorder is in good operating condition and is cleaned regularly.

Note: To cover processing and handling, there is a $10 fee for *any* returned check.

Insight for Living Catalog

Request a free copy of the Insight for Living catalog of books, tapes, and study guides by calling **1-800-772-8888** in the United States or **1-800-663-7639** in Canada.

Order Form

FET CS represents the entire *Faith That Endures . . . in Times like These* series in a special album cover, while FET 1–4 are the individual tapes included in the series. FET SG represents this study guide, should you desire to order additional copies.

Item	Calif.*	U.S.	B.C.*	Canada*	Quantity	Amount
		Unit Price				
FET CS	$31.32	$29.20	$36.60	$34.20		$
FET 1	6.76	6.30	7.61	7.23		
FET 2	6.76	6.30	7.61	7.23		
FET 3	6.76	6.30	7.61	7.23		
FET 4	6.76	6.30	7.61	7.23		
FET SG	4.26	3.95	5.08	5.08		
					Subtotal	
					Overseas Residents *Pay U.S. price plus 10% surface postage or 25% airmail.* *Also, see "How to Order by Mail."*	
					U.S. First-Class Shipping *For faster delivery, add 10% for postage and handling.*	
					Gift to Insight for Living *Tax-deductible in the United States and Canada.*	
					Total Amount Due *Please do not send cash.*	$

If there is a balance: ❑ Apply it as a donation ❑ Please refund
*These prices already include applicable taxes and shipping costs.

Payment by: ❑ Check or money order payable to Insight for Living ❑ Credit card

(Circle one): Visa MasterCard Discover Card Number_____

Expiration Date_____ Signature_____
We cannot process your credit card purchase without your signature.

Name_____

Address_____

City_____ State/Province_____

Zip/Postal Code_____ Country_____

Telephone (___)_____ Radio Station____ ____ ____ ____
If questions arise concerning your order, we may need to contact you.

Mail this order form to the Ordering Services Department at one of these addresses:
Insight for Living, Post Office Box 69000, Anaheim, CA 92817-0900
Insight for Living Ministries, Post Office Box 2510, Vancouver, BC, Canada V6B 3W7
Insight for Living, Inc., GPO Box 2823 EE, Melbourne, VIC 3001, Australia

Order Form

FET CS represents the entire *Faith That Endures . . . in Times like These* series in a special album cover, while FET 1–4 are the individual tapes included in the series. FET SG represents this study guide, should you desire to order additional copies.

Item	Calif.*	Unit Price U.S.	B.C.*	Canada*	Quantity	Amount
FET CS	$31.32	$29.20	$36.60	$34.20		$
FET 1	6.76	6.30	7.61	7.23		
FET 2	6.76	6.30	7.61	7.23		
FET 3	6.76	6.30	7.61	7.23		
FET 4	6.76	6.30	7.61	7.23		
FET SG	4.26	3.95	5.08	5.08		
					Subtotal	
				Overseas Residents *Pay U.S. price plus 10% surface postage or 25% airmail. Also, see "How to Order by Mail."*		
				U.S. First-Class Shipping *For faster delivery, add 10% for postage and handling.*		
				Gift to Insight for Living *Tax-deductible in the United States and Canada.*		
				Total Amount Due *Please do not send cash.*		$

If there is a balance: ❏ Apply it as a donation ❏ Please refund
*These prices already include applicable taxes and shipping costs.

Payment by: ❏ Check or money order payable to Insight for Living ❏ Credit card

(Circle one): Visa MasterCard Discover Card Number _____

Expiration Date_____ Signature_____
We cannot process your credit card purchase without your signature.

Name_____

Address_____

City_____ State/Province_____

Zip/Postal Code_____ Country_____

Telephone (___)_____ Radio Station____ ____ ____ ____
If questions arise concerning your order, we may need to contact you.

Mail this order form to the Ordering Services Department at one of these addresses:
Insight for Living, Post Office Box 69000, Anaheim, CA 92817-0900
Insight for Living Ministries, Post Office Box 2510, Vancouver, BC, Canada V6B 3W7
Insight for Living, Inc., GPO Box 2823 EE, Melbourne, VIC 3001, Australia

Order Form

FET CS represents the entire *Faith That Endures . . . in Times like These* series in a special album cover, while FET 1–4 are the individual tapes included in the series. FET SG represents this study guide, should you desire to order additional copies.

Item	Unit Price Calif.*	U.S.	B.C.*	Canada*	Quantity	Amount
FET CS	$31.32	$29.20	$36.60	$34.20		$
FET 1	6.76	6.30	7.61	7.23		
FET 2	6.76	6.30	7.61	7.23		
FET 3	6.76	6.30	7.61	7.23		
FET 4	6.76	6.30	7.61	7.23		
FET SG	4.26	3.95	5.08	5.08		
					Subtotal	
		Overseas Residents *Pay U.S. price plus 10% surface postage or 25% airmail. Also, see "How to Order by Mail."*				
		U.S. First-Class Shipping *For faster delivery, add 10% for postage and handling.*				
		Gift to Insight for Living *Tax-deductible in the United States and Canada.*				
		Total Amount Due *Please do not send cash.*				$

If there is a balance: ❏ Apply it as a donation ❏ Please refund
*These prices already include applicable taxes and shipping costs.

Payment by: ❏ Check or money order payable to Insight for Living ❏ Credit card

(Circle one): Visa   MasterCard   Discover Card   Number _____

Expiration Date_____   Signature_____
We cannot process your credit card purchase without your signature.

Name_____

Address_____

City_____   State/Province_____

Zip/Postal Code_____   Country_____

Telephone (___)_____   Radio Station____ ____ ____ ____
If questions arise concerning your order, we may need to contact you.

Mail this order form to the Ordering Services Department at one of these addresses:
Insight for Living, Post Office Box 69000, Anaheim, CA 92817-0900
Insight for Living Ministries, Post Office Box 2510, Vancouver, BC, Canada V6B 3W7
Insight for Living, Inc., GPO Box 2823 EE, Melbourne, VIC 3001, Australia